Second Edition

ESSENTIALS OF LEARNING FOR INSTRUCTION

Robert M. Gagné
Marcy Perkins Driscoll

Florida State University

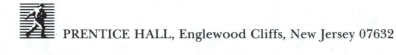

PRENTICE HALL, Englewood Cliffs, New Jersey 07632

Library of Congress Cataloging-in-Publication Data

GAGNÉ, ROBERT MILLS (date)
  Essentials of learning for instruction / Robert M.
Gagné, Marcy P. Driscoll.—2nd ed.
    p.   cm.
  Bibliography: p.
  Includes indexes.
  ISBN 0-13-286253-0
    1. Learning, Psychology of.   2. Learning.   3. Teaching.
I. Driscoll, Marcy P.   II. Title.
LB1060.G344   1989
370.15′2—dc19
                                        87-31188
                                        CIP

Editorial/production supervision: Linda B. Pawelchak
Cover design: Suzanne Bennett & Associates
Manufacturing buyer: Margaret Rizzi

 © 1988 by Prentice-Hall, Inc.
A Division of Simon & Schuster
Englewood Cliffs, New Jersey 07632

Printed in the United States of America

10 9 8 7 6 5

ISBN   0-13-286253-0

Prentice-Hall International (UK) Limited, *London*
Prentice-Hall of Australia Pty. Limited, *Sydney*
Prentice-Hall Canada Inc., *Toronto*
Prentice-Hall Hispanoamericana, S.A., *Mexico*
Prentice-Hall of India Private Limited, *New Delhi*
Prentice-Hall of Japan, Inc., *Tokyo*
Simon & Schuster Asia Pte. Ltd., *Singapore*
Editora Prentice-Hall do Brasil, Ltda., *Rio de Janeiro*

CONTENTS

PREFACE v

ONE
INTRODUCTION 1

Learning Theory 10
Topics of the Book 17
General References 19

TWO
THE PROCESSES OF LEARNING 21

The Processes of Learning in Sequence 24
Learning in Relation to Instruction 38
General References 41

THREE
THE OUTCOMES OF LEARNING 43

Types of Learning Outcomes 44
General References 61

FOUR
LEARNER MOTIVATION 63

Sources of Motivation for Learning 64
A Model of Motivation 67
Motivating the Learner 71
General References 81

FIVE
CONDITIONS FOR LEARNING 83

Categorizing Learning Outcomes 84
Learning Conditions 84
Learning Conditions in Instruction 103
General References 105

SIX

PLANNING INSTRUCTION   107

The Planning of Courses 108

Planning the Lesson 116

Self-Instruction and Learning 127

General References 131

SEVEN

LEARNER STRATEGIES   133

Strategies for Internal Processing 134

Strategies for Motivation 139

Acquisition of Learner Strategies 141

Implications for Teaching Learner
Strategies 144

Conclusion 147

General References 148

EIGHT

DELIVERING INSTRUCTION   151

Instruction in the Class 152

Instruction for the Individual Student 157

Using Audio and Visual Media 165

Some Summarizing Comments 172

General References 174

REFERENCES   175

INDEXES   181

PREFACE

This is a book about human learning, intended to be useful to teachers and prospective teachers. We have tried to write plainly about a complex subject, including the most basic facts and principles, and illustrating these with examples of learning in educational settings. We hope the contents of the book will provide a framework that can serve well in organizing thought and the accumulation of knowledge about teaching. In addition, we hope it will encourage students to seek additional knowledge about human learning as it applies to the design and conduct of instruction.

Learning is described here in terms of the information-processing model of learning and memory, a model that underlies many cognitive theories of learning. This model posits a number of internal processes that are subject to the influence of external events. The arrangement of external events to activate and support the internal processes of learning constitutes what is called *instruction*. The description of these external events and their effects on learning processes is the central theme of the book.

Initial chapters deal with learning principles and are followed by chapters describing applications to the planning and delivery of instruction. Revisions in this edition include new and up-to-date material in every chapter. Added new chapters deal with motivation for learning and with learner strategies.

We have continued the intent to use language that is concrete and to provide illustrations of the principles being discussed. The account describes what learning investigators have discovered only insofar as their findings illuminate the central theme. Our intention is to tell the prospective teacher, "This is what will be most helpful for you to know about human learning."

Embedded within each chapter are a number of self-study exercises composed of thought-provoking questions that serve the twin purposes of review and elaboration. These exercises provide occasional breaks for students studying the text and are expected to enhance retention of the contents. Each chapter contains a concluding section that summarizes and provides continuity with the succeeding chapter. General references at the end of each chapter, arranged by topics, can guide further study by the interested student. Specific references cited in the text are listed at the end of the book.

As a text, the book should find its greatest usefulness in undergraduate courses in educational psychology and as an adjunct to graduate offerings in this subject. It may also be appropriate as a supplementary text in courses in human learning, instructional methods, instructional design, and educational technology. In addition, the book may be a suitable component of courses and workshops offered as a part of the continuing education of teachers.

Robert M. Gagné
Marcy P. Driscoll
Tallahassee, Florida

ONE
INTRODUCTION

When students take part in an educational program, whether in school or some other setting, they are assumed to be engaged in *learning*. Their activities may be highly varied, since they may be learning many different things—how to read a book, how to analyze an economic problem, how to view a painting, how to play volleyball, and so forth. A person may become a student, and therefore be committed to learning, in any number of social contexts—a day care center, a public school, a college, an adult class, an on-the-job workshop, a correspondence course. Despite the variety of these situations, they share a primary aim: learning.

Thus, the central purpose of any program of education is to *promote learning*. This is true regardless of the age of the learners, the subject matter they are studying, or the context in which they are learning. Learning can occur from early childhood to extreme old age, and the number and kinds of things that can be learned in that time are incalculable. Educational institutions and programs aim to bring about learning of *particular* knowledge, skills, and attitudes. A kindergarten program, for example, may seek to teach children to be polite to one another, while an adult introductory class on computers may teach basic skills in programming.

Learning and the Teacher

Besides the student who is learning, the most important agent in an educational program is the teacher. The teacher is responsible for arranging the student's environment to promote learning. Sometimes, as in the primary grades, this task must be planned in careful detail, taking into account the limitations of attention and comprehension of the students. You may be familiar with the very short attention spans of young children. With older and more experienced students, teachers may plan conditions to promote learning in larger chunks. Older students will also take greater responsibility for their own learning and will provide for themselves those experiences that best help them learn. While the task of ensuring that learning occurs changes with the age and experience of the learners, it nonetheless remains an important part of the job of the teacher.

Teachers carry out the task of promoting learning by providing *instruction.* In fact, instruction may be defined as *the set of events designed to initiate, activate, and support learning* in a human learner. Such events must first be *planned;* second, they must be *delivered,* that is, made to have their effects on learners. For example, suppose you wanted to teach a class of first grade students some basic concepts such as *in front of, behind, above,* and *below.* You would plan what activities you would do as the teacher, such as introducing a pointing game, saying the words orally, and varying the objects you point to. You would also plan the activities the students would do, such as playing the pointing game, repeating the word, verifying the direction of pointing, and so on. Then you would deliver the instruction you had planned, which might go as follows: the children are assembled into a group, the various objects are identified, the group says each word in unison, then individual children take their turns determining the direction of pointing with you providing feedback, and so on.

The responsibilities of planning and delivering instruction obviously require a knowledge of the *process of learning.* In other words, in order to promote learning, a teacher must have some idea of what learning is and how it occurs. In order to plan events in the learner's environment which will activate and support learning, a teacher must gain a concept of what is going on "inside the learner's head." That is what knowledge of the principles of learning and learning theory provides. Sections of this chapter will introduce some of these concepts to you, and later chapters will expand on them.

The Nature of Learning

Learning is something that takes place inside a person's head—in the brain. Learning is called a *process* because it is formally comparable to other human organic processes such as digestion and respiration.

However, learning is an enormously intricate and complex process, which is only partially understood at present. As is true for other organic processes, knowledge about learning can be accumulated by scientific methods. When such knowledge is adequately verified, it can be expressed as *learning principles*. And when these principles appear to hang together in a way that makes rational sense, a *model* of the learning process can be constructed. Elaborations of this model (or of alternative models) are what are known as *learning theories*.

If learning is a process that occurs in a person's head, how can one know when, or if, it has occurred? This question is of obvious concern to a teacher, who must have some way of knowing when a student has learned. The answer is that learning is a process that enables organisms to modify their behavior fairly rapidly in a more or less permanent way, so that the same modification does not have to occur again and again in each new situation. Teachers, then, can recognize that learning has taken place when they note a *behavioral change* in the learner and also when they note the *persistence* of this change. In other words, teachers infer that learning has occurred from their observation of a permanent change in the learner's behavior.

There is, however, one major class of persistent behavioral change that is not learning and that is *maturation*—in other words, changes resulting from the growth of internal structures. The behavioral change that can be observed in an infant's use of her eyes, for example, or a child's progressive development of muscular coordination, are attributable to maturation. It is essential to distinguish these kinds of behavioral change from those called learning. Whereas learning typically occurs when an individual responds to and receives stimulation from the environment, maturation requires only internal growth. The persisting behavioral change called learning, then, must be confined to that which occurs when a person *interacts* with the external environment. As we shall see later, the capacity for learning reaches such a high level in human beings that certain types of interaction can be represented internally and therefore can take place entirely "in the head." For example, once you have learned numeric symbols for numbers of objects, you no longer need to interact with the objects themselves. You may represent internally their concepts and use these concepts for further learning.

Let's summarize what we have said about learning thus far. Learning is a *process* of which man and other animals are capable. It typically involves *interaction* with the external environment (or with a representation of this interaction, stored in the learner's memory). Learning is inferred when a change or *modification in behavior* occurs that *persists* over relatively long periods during the life of the individual. But how does learning actually occur? What are the internal processes involved in learning, and how are they influenced by events in the environment?

What kinds of human behavior can be modified by learning? What are the characteristics of the persisting states that result from learning? These are the major questions this book attempts to answer. In doing so, however, our orientation is a highly practical one. In other words, we intend to consider in some detail how a knowledge of learning can be applied to the planning and delivery of instruction.

Knowledge about Learning

Where does knowledge about learning come from? In other words, how are learning principles discovered and how are learning theories constructed? How is it known when a theory accurately and adequately represents learning? The answers to these questions lie in the *research* that is conducted about learning. Knowledge about learning comes from research on learning, research that may range from simple observations to elaborate, controlled experiments. Regardless of how facts about learning are obtained, they must be both *reliable* and *valid.* Facts are reliable when the same fact can be observed again and again under the same conditions; in other words, when it is dependable or consistent. To be valid, an item of knowledge must be applicable to a range of situations. It must not be so special that it occurs only in the situation in which it was first observed. In other words, if you observed some event but were not able to observe the event again when the circumstances were quite different, you would question whether what you observed the first time was real, or valid, as a principle.

Knowledge that is reliable and valid is obtained by scientific methods, by making controlled observations and verifying these observations. It might seem that a most economical way to obtain knowledge about learning would be to ask people how they learn. In general, however, learners are simply not aware of the internal processes that occur when they are learning and so cannot report them. Learners may be aware of some results of these processes or of some decisions made about these results. But when asked to report events of learning, people are usually unreliable; that is, their reports of these events vary from time to time and from learner to learner. For these reasons, learners' reports are not generally considered to be good sources of knowledge about learning.

In order to obtain sound knowledge about learning events, learning psychologists and educational researchers conduct various types of studies on learning. Psychologists are primarily interested in determining and describing the properties of learning and memory. Educational researchers may then use these results to make and verify predictions about the effects of various instructional methods and other external variables on learning.

Research that is either basic or applied begins with observations. Researchers make and record the results of observations as an initial step toward describing some phenomenon or event. After repeated observations, researchers have more confidence in the existence of the phenomenon and also have evidence about what factors are related to, or in some way influence, the phenomenon.

At this point, they may conduct *correlational studies*. With correlational studies, researchers are able to establish whether a relationship exists among observed events (referred to as *variables*) but not yet what this relationship may be. For example, suppose a researcher notes that children who watch a lot of television seem to know the meanings of more words than children who watch less television. To establish a relationship between the number of hours spent watching television and the number of words known, the researcher could record each of these quantities for a group of children and see how the numbers correspond. A positive relationship would result if the children, by and large, scored the same on both measures, that is, high on number of hours watched and high on number of words known, or low on hours watched and low on words known. A negative relationship would result if the children scored high on one measure but low on the other, for example, if they were high on number of hours watched but low on number of words known, or vice-versa. There would be no relationship if it appeared that the scores on the two measures did not systematically co-vary.

Let us suppose that the study showed a positive relationship between number of hours of television watched and number of words known. What could the researcher conclude? We hope you did *not* say that "watching television leads to a greater vocabulary"! At this point, the researcher knows only that television watching and size of vocabulary are *in some way* related. It may be that a third factor, such as parental involvement with the child, is actually responsible for the size of the child's vocabulary. The parent, for example, may watch television with the child, calling attention to and explaining unfamiliar words. Therefore, in order for researchers to conclude what variables influence a given phenomenon and how, they may conduct controlled *experimental* studies.

With experimental studies, researchers are able to determine what relationship exists among variables. They do this by presenting a specified set of materials to students in a situation controlled in specific ways and then observing the modifications in behavior brought about by the materials. From our aforementioned example, a researcher might now conduct an experimental study by having some parents interact with their children in specified ways while watching television together. The number of hours watched and the particular shows would be controlled, so that whatever change in vocabulary occurred could be attributed to the parent-child interaction.

Since direct observations on the *process* of learning cannot be made, researchers make inferences about this process from their observations of learners. These inferences give rise to generalized knowledge about learning. Researchers must then verify these learning principles. This is done by predicting additional learning outcomes to be observed in a newly specified situation, often with still another set of learners. When predicted outcomes correspond with observed outcomes, the principles are said to be verified, and such observations support the conclusion that the principles are valid.

An Example of the Study of Learning

Let us illustrate the procedures of gaining knowledge about learning with an example of a particular experimental study. The learning researchers in this case were interested in children learning the names and locations of the features of a map. To represent this kind of learning task, they constructed a map of a fictitious small town, including buildings, natural features, a set of railroad tracks, and several roads. Altogether there were eighteen features that could be identified and located. The map was drawn on a sheet of white paper about 13 inches square, and copies of this map were presented to the students at their desks.

Fifth grade students were told to study the map for 20 minutes, during which time they were to write about the features shown in the map (both natural and man-made), checking each feature off as they proceeded with their writing. The students were told they would be given a test on the contents of the map following this productive study period. At the end of 20 minutes, papers were collected and the students given a map-sized sheet showing only the railroad. They were then given 10 minutes to place as many features as they could remember on this sheet, paying special attention to their location.

Two different experimental groups were formed, twenty-four children in each; each group was given a different set of instructions for the writing phase of the activity. One group was instructed to write a geographic *description,* being sure to include where the features were located on the map and how they were spatially related to each other. In the other condition, learners were asked to write a *short story,* or *narrative,* about life in the town on the map (which was given the name *Hamlet*). Both groups were told to use each of the eighteen features in their description or narrative.

It was possible to score the maps produced by the students in two

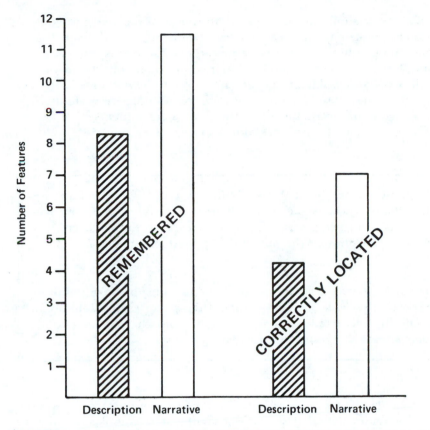
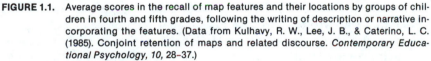

FIGURE 1.1.   Average scores in the recall of map features and their locations by groups of children in fourth and fifth grades, following the writing of description or narrative incorporating the features. (Data from Kulhavy, R. W., Lee, J. B., & Caterino, L. C. (1985). Conjoint retention of maps and related discourse. *Contemporary Educational Psychology, 10,* 28–37.)

different ways: for the number of features remembered, and for the number correctly located. The results are shown graphically in Figure 1.1. In the case of both measures of learning, children who studied by composing a narrative scored substantially higher than those who wrote a description.

Reliability.   The controlled observation of this study shows, then, that when fourth and fifth grade students are asked to remember map features by writing a story about them, they remember the features better than do students who are asked to write descriptions of them. Is this a *reliable* observation? This question is answered in the study, as is often customary, by using *repeated observations.* The investigators did not observe the learning of just one or two features; they observed as many as eighteen different features. A number this great increases confidence that the result is *replicable.* Taking two different measures, as was done in scoring maps for remembered features and for correct locations, is another circumstance that contributes to confidence in reliability. Two different measures have led to the same conclusion.

Suppose the results of this study turned out differently. Suppose the children who wrote narratives correctly *remembered* more features but correctly *located* fewer features than the children who wrote descriptions. What might this suggest about *reliability?*

Discussion: If such a result occurred, the investigators might want to repeat, or *replicate,* the study to see if the same result would occur again. If it occurred a second time, they would have greater confidence that their result was *replicable.*

Validity.   Is the conclusion about the effect of narrative versus descriptive writing a *valid* one? This is a slightly more complex question to answer. One answer comes from the observation that the learning scores of children who wrote a narrative were higher than those of (equivalent) children who wrote a description. How much higher were these scores, only a little or a great deal? In actuality, they were found to be *significantly* higher, as established by a statistical test that permits the investigator to reject the idea that such differences could have occurred by chance.

However, the question of validity concerns more than statistical significance. Would the principle about the superiority of narrative in aiding learning apply to any kind of map, any number of map features, or any kind of student? Obviously, we must be more cautious about validity when we are *generalizing* a set of conclusions. Additional studies with other observations will be needed to increase our confidence about the limits of applicability of the result. The principle is valid, but this is not an all-or-none matter; it is valid under conditions similar to those under which it was verified.

Controlling conditions.   The necessity for making controlled observations means that investigators of the learning process must make suitable arrangements for the selection of learners for their study and of the environment in which learning will occur. Sometimes the need for controls is such that they deal with individual learners in an isolated room, perhaps a laboratory room or a single learning carrel. On other occasions, as in the example just described, it is possible to conduct the study in one or more classrooms or in other assembly rooms within a school. The materials used to present the learning task must often be specially constructed in order to be appropriately controlled; in other instances, lessons presented in the normal course of instruction may be suitable. Often the most difficult factor to control in learning studies is the aptitude and learning background of the learners. When conducted in schools, studies usually require that a special effort be made to control so as to assure the *equivalence* of students in these characteristics. In the study described here, *random assignment* of students to the two different groups was the method employed to make the groups equivalent.

A principle of learning.   Besides the knowledge the map feature study yielded about the conditions of learning, was anything revealed about the internal *processes* that make learning happen? Again the answer is yes—but this answer must be carefully qualified. Making inferences about the processes of learning can seldom be confidently done from the results of a single study. What is suggested by this example is that facts are learned more readily when they can be meaningfully related by the learner to a kind of memory structure already possessed by the learner. In this case the structure is that of a *story.* The framework of a story is well known by the learners—a story has a beginning, an unfolding sequence of events, a high point of activity, and an ending. In contrast, the framework of a description has no such readily available points of reference. Thus it is easier for the learner to recall a set of facts (map features in this case) when these facts are learned within the highly familiar framework of a story.

Obviously, the existence of familiar frameworks (often called *schemas;* see Anderson, 1985) in learners' memories, as well as their properties for storing newly learned facts, must be inferred from a number of studies. Each study in a series may contribute some small amount of knowledge about the process of learning, while at the same time confirming other pieces of knowledge. (Additional examples of investigations of human learning are described in the books listed as General References at the end of this chapter.)

Let us suppose once again that the results of this study showed children who wrote narratives remembered more features but located fewer of them than children who wrote descriptions. How would this change the principle of learning suggested by the research?

Discussion: It might suggest that learning *types* of map features differs somehow from learning the *locations* of those features. If this were true, the conditions that facilitate learning types of features would likely be different from those that facilitate learning feature locations. Therefore, investigators would need to conduct further research to determine what specific conditions would best fit each type of learning.

LEARNING THEORY

The results of research on learning yield an accumulation of *learning principles* that can be repeatedly verified. These principles contribute to a body of knowledge about learning which continues to grow in breadth and precision. As knowledge grows, ways are suggested of organizing a number of disparate facts into a single conceptualization called a *theory.* A learning theory is designed to provide an explanation of several (sometimes many) specific facts that have been independently observed, by relating these facts to a conceptual *model.* The model itself cannot be directly observed, but it may generate a number of predictions that can be. To the extent that these predictions are verified, the learning theory becomes increasingly well established and more frequently employed as an explanation. When predictions are not verified, the learning theory may be modified to accommodate the observations, or, with an increasing number of observations that do not fit its predictions, the theory might be rejected in favor of a better one.

Behaviorist Learning Theory and the Technology of Behavior Modification

In 1913, a leading investigator of learning, E. L. Thorndike, proposed what later came to be known as a fundamental law of psychology. He called it the Law of Effect and expressed it as follows:

> When a modifiable connection between a single situation and a response is made and is accompanied by a satisfying state of affairs, that connection's strength is increased. When made and accompanied by an annoying state of affairs, its strength is decreased. (Thorndike, 1913, p. 4)

B. F. Skinner, in the early 1950s, restated this law as *reinforcement* and developed a general behaviorist theory of learning which incorporated it. His is called a *behaviorist theory* because Skinner proposed that learning could be understood and described by studying only overt behavior and its consequences in the environment. A behavior became learned, for example, when its occurrence led to a satisfying result, or was *reinforced*. This satisfying consequence, or reinforcement, made it more likely that the organism would repeat the behavior.

All of the principles that comprise Skinner's theory, then, relate the learner's behavior directly to external events in the environment. They make no assumptions about or reference to the internal processes that may go on within learners as they learn. This is *not* to say that behaviorists denied the existence of such processes; rather, they believed learning could be adequately described and influenced without reference to such processes.

Behaviorist theory has persisted for many years and has been shown to have validity under many conditions. Most notably, the technology of behavior modification has been shown to be highly effective in such areas as classroom discipline, personal self-control (as in controlling one's weight, stopping smoking, and so forth), and teaching self-mainte- nance skills to mentally retarded individuals. In each of these situations, desirable and undesirable behaviors are defined and procedures under- taken to increase the frequency of desirable behaviors and decrease the occurrence of undesirable behaviors. The procedures themselves are de- rived from Skinner's laws of reinforcement. For a simple example, con- sider the child who consistently disrupts class by getting out of her seat and distracting the teacher. In this case, "getting out of seat" is undesir- able and must be reduced in frequency, while "staying in seat" is consid- ered desirable and so must be increased in frequency. To do this, the teacher might ignore "getting out of seat" (removing the reinforcement) to *extinguish* this behavior, while at the same time giving the child extra attention when she is in her seat, thus reinforcing "staying in seat."

While behaviorist theory has certainly contributed a great deal to our understanding of learning, evidence has been obtained that suggests there is more to learning than what behaviorist theory is able to describe. Moreover, more recent conceptions of learning, by considering "what goes on inside a learner's head," have been able to offer reasonable explanations for *why* behaviorist principles may or may not work in given situations. Thus, from accumulating evidence and periodic questioning of assumptions, learning theory assumes new forms over the years.

Modern Learning Theory and Its Model

The theory of learning displayed in this book is of a cognitive variety known as *information-processing theory.* According to this type of theory, the processes that are presumed to account for learning make certain kinds of *transformations* of *inputs* to *outputs* in a fashion somewhat analogous to the workings of a computer. For example, when you are in a learning situation, physical stimulation of your eyes, ears, and other senses is transformed into neural messages. These messages then undergo other transformations in the nervous system so that they can be stored and later recalled. The recalled information is again transformed into still other kinds of messages that control the action of your muscles. The result is speech or other types of movement indicating that you have learned some performance. These various forms of transformation are called *learning processes;* they are what goes on "inside the learner's head." It is these processes, their characteristics, and their manner of functioning that constitute the essence of modern cognitive learning theory.

A basic model of learning and memory, representing the essential features of most cognitive learning theories, is shown in Figure 1.2. The model shows the structures postulated to exist in the central nervous system of the learner. These structures are presumed to be neural networks, and the processes that transform information are presumed to be electrochemical in nature. No precise locations for these structures and processes have yet been determined (see Lindsay & Norman, 1977). Rather, the model serves to represent learning as best we know it and enables us to derive implications for instruction that are empirically verifiable.

The model shown in Figure 1.2 is the basis for our discussion of learning processes and their implications for instruction in the later chapters of this book. At this point, we do not expect you to acquire a full understanding of the model, just an acquaintance with its major features. Try to get a mental picture of Figure 1.2, so that you can follow the *flow* of information and capture the idea that it is *processed* (transformed) in various ways as it passes from one structure to another.

The Flow of Information

Stimulation from the *environment* affects a learner's *receptors* and enters the nervous system via a *sensory register.* You have visual receptors, auditory receptors, taste receptors, and so forth, and for each type of receptor, a sensory register is responsible for the initial perception of

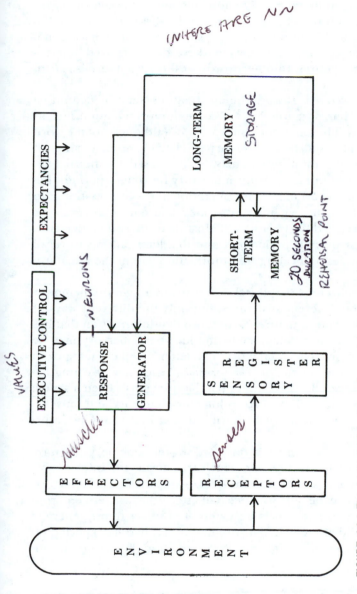

FIGURE 1.2. The basic model of learning and memory underlying modern information-processing theories.

information coming to that sense. The information in the sensory register has the form of a representation of the original stimulation. The information remains in this form for only the smallest fraction of a second. It is perceived as objects and shapes, when these are recognized in terms of their prominent features. In other words, at this stage there is *pattern recognition.*

Entering the *short-term memory,* the information is now coded into a conceptual form. Thus, a figure like X becomes a representation such as an "X"; a figure like II becomes the concept "two" (although not the word *two*). Persistence in the short-term memory is relatively brief, a matter of seconds. However, the information may be processed by internal rehearsal and preserved in the short-term memory for longer periods. Rehearsal may also play a part in another operation: if the information is to be remembered, it is once again transformed and enters the *long-term memory,* where it is stored for later recall. Most theories assume that storage in long-term memory is permanent and that later failures to recall result from difficulties of locating the information within the long-term memory.

It is important to note that the short-term and long-term memories may not actually be different structures, but only the different ways of functioning for the same structure. Notice also that information that has passed from the short-term memory to the long-term memory may be *retrieved* back to the short-term memory. The latter is sometimes spoken of as the *working memory* or the *conscious memory.* When new learning depends partly on the recall of something that has previously been learned, this something must be retrieved from long-term memory and must reenter the short-term memory, where it will interact with incoming information.

Information from either short-term or long-term memory, when retrieved, passes to a *response generator,* which transforms the information into a neural message to activate the *effectors* (muscles). The effectors, then, actually produce the performance that affects the learner's environment. This action is what enables an external observer (most generally the teacher) to tell that the original stimulation has had its expected effect—that the "information has been processed," and the learner has indeed learned.

The control of processing.   A very important set of structures shown in Figure 1.2 has yet to be described. These are labeled *executive control* and *expectancies.* Signals from these structures are presumed to activate and modify the overall flow of information. For example, in any learning situation, you have an expectancy of what you will be able to do once you have learned. Your expectancy affects how you perceive an external stimulus, how you code it in memory, and how you transform it into action. Think how differently you approach a task if you know you must recall it verbatim or just recognize the main points. Similarly, *control processes* originating in the executive control structure may determine how the information is coded when it enters long-term memory and how the search and retrieval are conducted for recall, among other things. (References to various theoretical accounts are given at the end of this chapter.)

The ways in which learning occurs are critically influenced by processes initiated in the executive control and expectancy structures. The *flow* of information is one aspect of the learning model—the *control* of this flow, which determines the transformations the information undergoes, is quite another. In later chapters, we shall have more to say about expectancies and also about control processes, which we refer to as *cognitive strategies*.

A note about learning theory. A learning theory attempts to postulate as few different processes as possible and to endow each with as few properties as possible, while still managing to explain the phenomena of learning. In this sense, it is generally thought that the simplest theory is the best. However, the simplest model may not always be adequate to explain the phenomena to which it is addressed. When this happens, the learning theorist faces the necessity of adding features to the model or choosing a more complex model. There is always a justifiable reluctance to do this since the loss of simplicity brings with it a loss of clarity and explanatory power.

While behavioral theory occupies a prominent place in research on learning, and it has been the source of many important applications in education, it nonetheless fails to account for many observations about learning. Moreover, many important questions about learning that cognitive theorists are now confronting would not even be raised by theorists from a behavioral perspective. Therefore, the newer theory represented here is in greater accord with observations of learning and thus is more widely accepted despite its relative loss of simplicity.

The Usefulness of Learning Theory

Of what use is learning theory to you, the teacher or prospective teacher? How can it help in the day-to-day performance of the many tasks you are expected to do? These important questions deserve to be considered and answered by those who choose teaching as a profession. Since the promotion of learning is still the central purpose of educational programs, it is a central responsibility of the teachers involved in these programs. How can learning theory help teachers promote learning?

First of all, it is possible to have false expectations concerning the application of learning principles and learning theory to the job of teaching. One irrational expectation is that teachers can apply their knowledge of learning to virtually *all* aspects of designing lessons and conducting classes. It is easy to show that this cannot be the case. Suppose you teach in a classroom in which the desks are bolted to the floor or the chalkboards are beyond the reach of all but your tallest students. It is your practical knowledge of the constraints and possible alternatives to them that will guide you in making decisions about class activities, as well as your knowledge of learning theory.

Another kind of false expectation about the application of learning theory is the notion that the right theory or principle will provide a "magic key" to teaching. In other words, the right theory will tell you what to do in all situations. However, the variety of situations that characterize instruction make it impossible for a theory with general applicability to determine the details of instructional procedures in a constant fashion. Sometimes, for example, repetition is a procedure that promotes learning; sometimes it does not. Sometimes it is valuable to ask students to learn new concepts by discovering them; sometimes it is better to tell what the concepts are. And in certain cases, learning is better promoted by asking questions of students; on other occasions it may be better to have students formulate their own questions. An understanding of learning theory does not lead to the use of standardized procedures, nor is it likely to furnish a single best procedure that can be applied in all teaching situations.

On the other hand, the following points outline what a knowledge of learning theory *can* reasonably be expected to do for a teacher:

1. In the *planning* of lessons and courses, learning principles disclose the limits of what is possible in instruction. For example, suppose you were teaching students to spell new words. According to theory, practicing on words whose spellings are familiar to the learners will *not* help them on new words. Therefore, regardless of what other conditions may be present, you would know from learning theory that this procedure could be ruled out immediately.

2. In the *conduct* of instruction, a knowledge of learning theory can guide the teacher's choice of action. For example, if a course in American Government asks students to learn what people's right is specified by the fourth amendment to the U.S. Constitution, the teacher needs to consider how the essential meaning of this amendment can best be presented. Analyzing the situation to discover what learning is needed is a first step in determining what instruction ought to be given. Learning theory provides the knowledge of what alternatives are possible and how they may be undertaken to promote the necessary learning.

3. In *assessing* what has been learned, principles of learning make possible the means of comparing what students are able to do with what they were expected to have learned. For example, if you expected students to have learned how to calculate an average of a set of numbers, knowing learning principles would enable you to use procedures that will reveal whether students had learned the skill or not. Obviously, asking the question, "Do you know what an average is?" or "Do you know how to calculate an average?" will not accomplish the purpose. Rather, you would give them groups of numbers and ask them to calculate the averages. The kinds of questions, and the kinds of student performances, that are capable of assessing such learning can be derived from verified learning principles.

These uses of knowledge of theories and principles of learning demonstrate that such knowledge guides the various activities of the teacher in planning and managing instruction. While learning theory cannot be expected to determine step-by-step procedures, it nevertheless provides direction, options, and priorities for the teacher's actions. When you verify your activities against the standards of learning theory, you accomplish two highly desirable things. First, you avoid any grossly inappropriate actions that, although seemingly desirable on other grounds, nevertheless fail to promote learning in students. And second, you adopt and maintain attitudes that support learning as the central purpose of your activities. In the face of many potential distractions in the practice of teaching, you succeed in keeping student learning as a primary focus of concern.

TOPICS OF THE BOOK

As people concerned with the selection of instructional materials and the design, management, and evaluation of instruction, teachers are aided by their knowledge of learning principles and theories. It is the purpose of this book to convey this knowledge in the most fundamental sense. Of course, we cannot describe all there is to know about learning since that would require many books. However, as we indicated earlier in this chapter, the essentials that you, as teachers, need to know are treated as follows in this volume:

1. What is meant by learning, how knowledge of learning is obtained, and the basic model underlying modern learning theories have been described in this chapter. In addition, we have tried to show why such knowledge is of value to teachers in the various roles they perform and to suggest how such knowledge can be used to guide the planning and conduct of instruction.

2. The next topic to be considered, in Chapter 2, is the *processes* involved in learning. What takes place inside learners when learning occurs? What kinds of events take place in the environment that provide support for learning? Given the existence of these processes with their accompanying external events, what can be said about arranging conditions to promote learning?

3. What kinds of performances do people learn? In Chapter 3 we will consider the kinds of performances people are capable of learning, called *learning outcomes*. In addition, the implications of these principles for identifying classes of learning *objectives* are described.

4. In a fourth chapter, we give an account of the sources of learner motivation. A model of motivation for learning called the ARCS system is described, with its component factors of attention, relevance, confidence, and satisfaction. These four conditions are related to procedures of the learning situation.

5. Having distinguished the outcomes of learning, we proceed in Chapter 5 to deal with such questions as: What conditions, in addition to suitable motivation, are necessary to bring about learning aimed at each of these types of outcomes? What can be done to make learning effective and also efficient? Other questions dealt with in this chapter pertain to the conditions affecting the retention of learning and the transfer of learning to other tasks and situations.

6. How can knowledge of learning principles be used in planning instruction? This is the subject of Chapter 6, which considers topic and lesson planning in terms of the events within a lesson. Planning is based on the objectives of instruction and the arrangement of instructional events to activate and support learning processes.

7. A particular aspect of instructional planning concerns the question of providing cognitive strategies that can be acquired and used by the learner. In Chapter 7, we describe learner strategies that can be used by students to control their own learning processes. These include techniques for control of information processing and also of emotional states that may influence learning.

8. Chapter 8 discusses the various learning situations in which the delivery of instruction may be accomplished. Questions considered pertain to the employment of instructional events in self-instruction, in tutoring in the class, and the contrasts that these situations provide. Other comparisons among delivery systems arise from the use of different media for instruction and in their differential effectiveness for supporting learning processes.

The purpose of the book as a whole should by now be clear. It is to describe essential principles of learning. This is done in order to provide teachers or prospective teachers with knowledge useful in the selection and design of instructional procedures and materials, the management of instruction, and the assessment of its outcomes. All these areas of teacher decision-making relate to the promotion of learning.

A note about exercises.   Throughout the chapters of this book, we have provided practice exercises to help you learn and apply the principles we describe. In these exercises we have tried to include examples from a wide variety of subjects and teaching situations so that, regardless of your area of interest, you will find it easy to implement these principles in your own teaching.

A note about references.   At the end of each chapter are listed a number of references related to the topics discussed. These are books or general articles that will enable you to investigate more thoroughly matters of special interest to you. In addition, specific references cited in the text are listed at the end of the book.

GENERAL REFERENCES

Theories of Learning

Bower, G. H., & Hilgard, E. R. (1981). *Theories of learning,* 5th ed. Englewood Cliffs, NJ: Prentice Hall.
Hill, W. F. (1981). *Principles of learning: A handbook of applications.* Palo Alto, CA: Mayfield.

Information Processing

Bransford, J. D. (1979). *Human cognition.* Belmont, CA: Wadsworth.
Klatzky, R. L. (1980). *Human memory: Structures and processes,* 2nd ed. San Francisco: Freeman.
Lindsay, P. H., & Norman, D. A. (1977). *Human information processing: An introduction to psychology,* 2nd ed. New York: Academic Press.

Learning and Instruction

Gagné, R. M., Briggs, L. J., & Wager, W. W. (1988). *Principles of instructional design,* 3rd ed. New York: Holt, Rinehart and Winston.
Reigeluth, C. M. (Ed.). (1983). *Instructional-design theories and models: An overview of their current status.* Hillsdale, NJ: Erlbaum.

TWO
THE PROCESSES
OF LEARNING

As indicated by the model introduced in Chapter 1, learning occurs as a result of the interaction of an individual and the environment. An observer knows that learning has taken place when the learner's performance can be seen to have changed. At one moment in time, for example, a child may not be able to point to a pyramid among a group of objects when asked the question, "Where is the pyramid?" When the pyramid is then indicated and its name given, an opportunity is provided for the interaction called learning to take place. Later, the question is again asked, and the child now identifies the object. By means of this set of observations, the change in the child's behavior and a *persistence* of this change is seen, and the inference can be made that *learning* has taken place.

The set of events observed as learning is formally similar whether we are speaking of changes in the performances of riding a bicycle, recounting the provisions of the Dred Scott decision, cooking peanut brittle, composing a grammatically correct sentence, solving a differential equation, or interpreting a building code. Countless performances are modified during the course of a person's life, and most of these changes result from learning. The kinds of performances themselves vary greatly, as do the situations in which they occur; yet we may identify and describe some common features of the events of learning. In this chapter, we will consider these common features and see what they imply for teaching.

Some of the events that make up a learning incident are external to learners. These are the readily observable things: the stimulation that reaches learners and the products (including written and spoken information) that result from their responding. In addition, many learning events are internal to learners and are inferred from the observations made externally. These internal activities, which are considered to take place in a learner's central nervous system, are called *processes of learning*. These processes are implied by the transition points between each set of structures of the basic learning model shown in Chapter 1 (Figure 1.2). These processes transform the initial stimulation arising in the environment into the internal events that produce a change in a learner's performance. Remember it is this change in performance that permits the inference that learning has occurred.

Learning Processes

Let us look more closely at the processes that transpire when learning takes place. The typical processes that make up a single act of learning are shown in Figure 2.1. The figure follows the original model in implying that these processes occur in sequence. (Indeed, the processes may best be conceived as forming a sequence, although some learning theories allow for simultaneous or *parallel processing*.) Stimulation of a learner's receptors leads to *reception* of sensory patterns that are briefly registered in a sensory register. This information is next processed by *selective perception* of its prominent features. Now the information is ready for *short-term storage,* and for the *rehearsal* that preserves it for a short while, preparatory to its entry into *long-term memory.* Of critical importance is the next process of *semantic encoding,* which transforms the information into the meaningful form that it takes in long-term memory. By meaningful here is meant having a subject and a predicate, as in the sentence "Columbus discovered America."

It is when information is processed as long-term storage that we can see the first evidence that learning has occurred. For a response to be made, in other words, there must be processes in *search* and *retrieval* to activate the response generator, which leads to the *performance* that verifies the existence of learning. When learners observe the results of their performance, they receive *feedback,* which gives rise to *reinforcement,* having internal effects on the entire learning act.

The processes of learning shown in Figure 2.1 cannot necessarily be observed under everyday circumstances. Special experimental controls and specially designed learning situations are necessary in order to study any one or any combination of the processes in terms of their sepa-

STRUCTURE

PROCESS

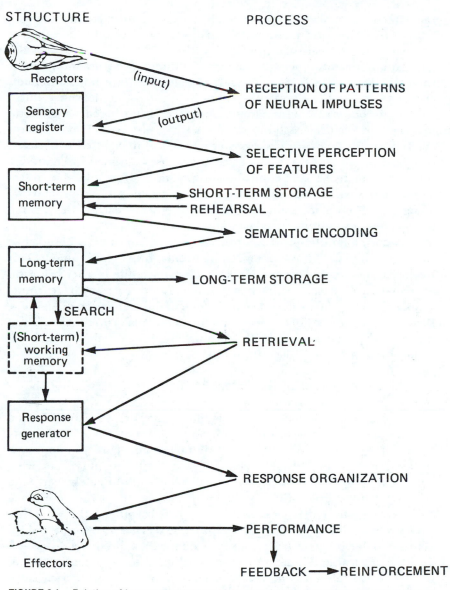

FIGURE 2.1.   Relation of learner structures and processes in an act of learning. (From Gagné, R. M., *The conditions of learning,* 4th ed. New York: Holt, Rinehart and Winston, 1985. Reproduced by permission of the copyright owner, Holt, Rinehart and Winston.)

rate effects on an act of learning. Such study, of course, is often the purpose of scientific investigations of learning that lead to more complete
understanding of learning processes.

Another caution needs to be made in interpreting the information
shown in Figure 2.1. This is the fact that learners are not aware, and
apparently cannot be aware, of most of the processes of learning. Intro-
spective accounts of what is happening internally during an act of learning have not been successful in revealing these processes. Usually, learners' reports of their own processes are quite uninformative. It needs to
be borne in mind that the processes and phases outlined in Figure 2.1
result from many years of controlled observations of people who are engaged in learning, followed by rational construction of "what must be
going on." These conclusions could not have been reached by learning
investigators examining their own minds.

Even though the processes of learning are not directly observable,
they nevertheless can be influenced by events in the environment. This
is what a *learning situation* amounts to in practice: the teacher brings to
bear certain external factors that influence the processes of learning.
Thus, events may be made to occur that affect the motivation of learners,
their attention, or any of the other processes that make up the total learning act. When used to promote learning, these external influences together constitute the procedures of *instruction*.

Executive control and expectancies.   Other processes, not shown
in Figure 2.1, consist of those that give learners control over how information is managed in learning and memory; they are accordingly called
executive control processes (Atkinson & Shiffrin, 1968). For example, suppose you are reading a technical article on science. How you approach
the task, that is, what strategies you employ to help you understand what
you are reading, will influence or *control* what you ultimately learn and
remember from the article. Also included in this category are the *expectancies* learners have of what the results of their learning will be. In other
words, when a teacher tells you what is to be learned, or you decide for
yourself, based on your own reasoning, you have acquired certain expectancies for learning. These expectancies will tend to influence a number
of processes while learning is taking place and will provide a basis for
satisfaction when learning is completed.

THE PROCESSES OF LEARNING IN SEQUENCE

It is convenient to think of a single act of learning as a set of events
occurring in sequence. As previously noted, such a sequence is not fixed

or invariable, since the parallel occurrence of some processes may take place. However, considering a learning act as a whole, it is evident that some events must occur before others, and we can best describe them in that fashion.

Motivation as Preparation for Learning

It is a truism that in order for learning to occur, one must have a motivated individual. But there are many forms of motivation, some of which are relevant to learning and instruction, and others which are not. For the promotion of learning, we must deal primarily with *incentive motivation,* a type of motivation in which the individual strives to achieve some goal and is in some way rewarded for reaching it. Incentive motivation is involved in many school and classroom situations. If you have begun a project on Greek sculpture, you want to achieve the goal of completing it. Or, once you have begun to solve simultaneous algebraic equations, you want to be able to do all such problems correctly, that is, to attain an answer that will check out. Youngsters in the first grade want to learn about the strange new shell their classmate is showing and describing, because they can then ask a "good" question about it, or perhaps later tell their parents about it.

Incentive motivation has been called by a variety of names, including *achievement motivation, effectance,* and the *urge for mastery.* Some psychologists view it as a fundamental human urge, one that is broadly involved in the behavior of human beings (White, 1959). Presumably, it reflects the natural tendency of humans to manipulate, dominate, and "master" their environment. This is what people do when they make something, rearrange things, complete something they have fabricated, or create something that did not previously exist. For the learning that takes place in the educational environment, the goals that are possible to achieve are many and varied—completing a problem, printing a message, writing an essay, constructing a model of a city, making a high score in a basketball game. All these activities may lead to achievable goals that engender learning.

Establishing motivation. On some occasions, however, learners may not be initially motivated by the incentive of achieving a goal. In these cases, the second alternative to action comes into play: one must establish the motivation, rather than simply verify that it is present. As is implied by Figure 2.1, motivation may be established by generating within learners an expectancy, an anticipation of the reward they will obtain when they achieve some goal (Estes, 1972). This expectancy can be established by telling learners what they can expect to happen as a consequence of their learning activity. For example, you may be told that when your learning is completed, you will be able to distinguish good art from bad, to read sentences in Spanish, or to repair a television set.

Sometimes, however, learners must acquire the desired expectancy by learning, rather than by simply being told. This is particularly true for younger learners, for whom communicating the incentive may not be sufficiently effective to establish motivation. The expectancy may need to be learned in a more direct way. Learners acquire an expectancy when their attainment of a goal is rewarded. In order to generate such expectancies, situations can be arranged that permit learners to reach intended goals before they have actually acquired necessary skills. Thus, one can guide a student through the steps of a mathematics problem and then show her that she has found the answer. This situation provides a reward and consequently tends to generate an expectancy that will motivate the student to learn how to solve such problems. As another example, one can help a child to form the initial letter of his name by doing most of it for him and then allowing him to complete it. By this means, one rewards the child for an accomplishment, and this in turn helps to establish the expectancy of this accomplishment.

Establishing an appropriate expectancy for learning is sometimes a matter of *channeling* preexisting motivation in a new direction. A child, for example, may be motivated to become an adult, and therefore to engage in adult activities. An adultlike responsibility, such as tutoring another child, may be an activity in which he participates with enthusiasm. Obviously, he must learn something well before he can engage in tutoring. The teacher can make the tutoring contingent upon his demonstrated mastery of a lesson or subject (cf. Skinner, 1968). The likely result is that he will acquire newly invigorated expectancies for achievement through his own learning.

These and other means can be employed to generate expectancies in learners, and thus to establish new forms of motivation that are not initially present. It should be emphasized, however, that the acquiring of an expectancy does not itself complete the learning; instead, it simply prepares the way for the learning that is to follow. Establishing motivation is a preparatory phase for an act of learning.

Attention

As Figure 2.1 indicates, *reception* of stimuli is the initial event in the learning sequence. A motivated learner must first receive the stimulation that will, after being transformed, enter into the essential learning incident and be stored in memory. The learner must, in other words, *attend* to the parts of the total stimulation that are relevant to the learning about to be undertaken.

To review, motivated learners are those who want to achieve some goal, such as drawing a picture, cultivating an ant colony, completing a laboratory experiment, or sailing a small boat. And learning occurs as students work toward attaining these goals. Can you name examples from your own experience in which learners (including yourself) were motivated to achieve a goal?

When learners are not already motivated toward achieving the goals a teacher has in mind, she may establish motivation by creating an expectancy of learning. What are examples of ways she might do this?

Some other examples are:

> Telling a first grade class they will be able to make change for one dollar.
> Telling education students they will be able to write good test items.
> Showing students a dance movement they will be learning how to perform.
> Telling a student he may use the computer to complete a writing assignment.

The process of attention is usually conceived as a temporary internal state, called a *mental set,* or simply a *set* (Hebb, 1972). Once established, a set operates as one kind of executive control process (Figure 1.2). A set to attend may be activated by external stimulation and persist over a limited period of time alerting the individual to receive certain kinds of stimulation. "Listen to the next two words I say, to see if they are different" serves to establish an attentional set. Attention may be initially captured by sudden changes in stimulation, a principle used in advertising displays and in motion pictures by abrupt cutting from one scene to another. In textbooks, attention is caught by varying sizes of type, by interspersing pictures, and by many other means of varying the pattern of stimulation presented. The teacher has available a number of means of influencing attention—changes in intensity of speaking, movements of the arms and head, and many others.

Usually, children in the early grades must learn to direct their attention in response to verbal communications. Although they may initially attend to a picture shown in a workbook, children must also learn to respond appropriately to such verbal directions as "Look at the upper part of this picture," or "Notice the letter under this picture." Oral or printed directions of this sort may come to control attention over the course of several learning acts. In some instances, however, special efforts need to be made to ensure that this early phase of learning—attending— has itself been learned. As learners gain in experience, the control of attention by oral or printed directions becomes virtually an automatic feature of their behavior.

Selective Perception of Features

The extremely brief registration that takes place in sensory registers is a fairly undifferentiated total impression of external stimulation. Now, guided in part by an expectancy and an attentional set, a learner must *perceive* the aspects of stimulation relevant to learning. When instruction has been deliberately planned, the learner is presented with stimuli that must be used in learning. For example, if the object of learning is com- puting areas of rectangles, then rectangular figures and their dimensions are presented; if the aim is learning to converse in French, then orally spoken French sentences are presented; and so on. The stimuli that are presented are directly related to the learning task. Furthermore, their relevant features are presented so as to form a pattern, as opposed to an unorganized jumble of impressions. As a result, what is accomplished is *selective perception* (sometimes called *pattern recognition;* see Anderson, 1985; Klatzky, 1980).

Guided by the pattern of features presented, by verbal directions, and by previous learning, learners selectively perceive the external stim- ulation that is relevant to the learning goal they have in mind. For exam- ple, as you read this, you perceive the words on a printed page, not the composition of the print and paper; you also perceive the form of a printed triangle shown in an example, not the thickness of its lines. Given a different expectancy for a different learning goal, you might perceive the type of print rather than the words, or the characteristics of the lines rather than the form of the triangle. Perception is *selective,* as influenced by the features of stimulation presented, by the expectancy adopted, and by verbal directions that reflect the particular goal of learn- ing. Of course, it is common for experienced learners to give themselves directions and thus control their own perception processes. For example, if you are a music student learning to play the trombone, you might spe- cifically listen for, and perceive, the trombone part in an orchestral per- formance.

In order for selective perception to be possible, the various features of external stimulation must be distinguished or *discriminated.* Although many discriminations have been learned by children by the time they attain school age, some may not have been, and this fact establishes the need for *perceptual learning* (Gibson, 1968). For example, children in kindergarten or first grade may not yet have learned to perceive a printed *d* as different from a printed *b*; they look the same. In hearing musical sounds, they may not yet have learned to discriminate the progressions sol–fa and fa–sol. Thus, before further learning can occur, children may need to learn to discriminate, that is, to perceive selectively the features of external stimulation that enter into other acts of learning.

Teachers have available to them a variety of means to direct attention and influence selective perception in order to facilitate the learning of a particular goal. For examples below, indicate whether *attention* or *selective perception* is the process most likely to be influenced.

_____ 1. Children are learning the concept of "smooth." The teacher brings in paper and cloth of varying textures for them to feel.

_____ 2. Music students are learning to identify changes in rhythm in various musical selections. The teacher says, "Now listen carefully to the next four bars."

_____ 3. Definitions of key vocabulary in a psychology textbook are highlighted in boldface print.

_____ 4. Pictures and their accompanying word labels appear in a first grade basal reader to illustrate the new words to be learned.

Answers: (1) selective perception; (2) attention; (3) selective perception; (4) selective perception

---

Storage in short-term memory.   What becomes stored in the short-term memory is apparently not exactly the same as what has been perceived. There is a *transformation* of the perceived entity into a form that is recognizable to a learner and most readily storable. The existence of this process is revealed by studies which show that, generally speaking, what is immediately remembered is almost never exactly the same as what was originally displayed. The material presented is sometimes distorted in certain ways, sometimes simplified or *regularized,* and sometimes embellished. What is stored in the short-term memory is apparently not an exact representation or "mental picture" of what was seen or heard.

A number of instances of this transformational process can be found in reports on studies of learning. For example, when individuals

in a laboratory experiment were asked to learn the shapes of simple figures and later asked to draw them, their reproductions showed a number
of kinds of alterations tending to make the figures simpler and more
symmetrical (Gibson, 1929). Two of these figures and several of their reproductions are shown in Figure 2.2. The changes in the figures presumably occurred when they were processed for short-term storage by the
learners, each in a somewhat different way. It is notable, though, that in
all cases the *essential features* of the figures were preserved.

How do words and verbal messages get stored in short-term memory? It has been found that confusions among words in short-term memory occur on the basis of their sounds, as opposed to either their appear-
ances or their meanings (Conrad, 1964). Even when words, numerals, or
phrases are presented visually, confusions among them take place on the
basis of their sounds. That is to say, immediate memory for a word like
ship is more likely to show confusion with *slip* (which has a similar sound)
than with *boat* (which is similar in meaning). In telephone numbers, the
numeral *9* tends to be confused with *5* because their sounds are similar.
Much of the storage in short-term memory is of this *acoustic* sort.

Rehearsal and chunking.   The capacity of the short-term memory
is limited in two different ways. First, the length of time items can remain
stored without additional processing is approximately 20 seconds (Anderson, 1985; Peterson & Peterson, 1959). And second, the number of
individual items that can be stored is limited to a few (seven, or perhaps
fewer).

A way of overcoming the time limitation of short-term memory is
by *rehearsal,* covertly saying things over to oneself. You will be familiar
with this method of keeping a telephone number in mind after looking

FIGURE 2.2.   Original figures and reproductions of them made by several different learners.
(From Gibson, J. J. The reproduction of visually perceived forms. *Journal of Experimental Psychology*, 1929, *12*, 1–39.)

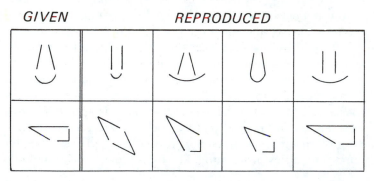

GIVEN   REPRODUCED

it up. Rehearsal can extend the time of short-term memory more or less indefinitely, or until one gets tired of it. Other examples of rehearsal are found in many school tasks. For example, in changing several fractions to those having a common denominator, that denominator itself may have to be renewed by rehearsal while various other operations (division, multiplication) are carried out.

The capacity of short-term memory is limited; for example, if you ask adult learners to repeat back immediately a set of individual letters or numerals (called the *immediate memory span*), the learners are usually capable of repeating back seven plus or minus two (Miller, 1956). Therefore, we expect people to be able to store, in this short-term sense, a set of seven letters like:

B P N C R L W

However, if the following set were to be presented:

F B I R C A I R S U P S

twelve letters could obviously be easily remembered by perceiving them as four triplets. This kind of processing is called *chunking;* it is a frequent and familiar kind of transformation that takes place in short-term memory.

By means of these processes of rehearsal and chunking, we are able to store information temporarily and to have it readily available as a basis for performance, prepared for storage in long-term memory and also for interaction with other incoming information. The short-term memory thus deals with highly active information processing. In recognition of its important functions, it is often referred to as *working memory.*

Semantic Encoding

While the short-term memory has several processing operations relating directly to human performance, one of its most essential functions is as a junction for input to the long-term memory. At this busy junction, incoming information is prepared for entry into long-term storage. The processes of rehearsal and chunking operate on new information as one would expect. But in addition, the preparation for long-term storage includes *encoding,* usually of the sort called *semantic encoding.* One or another kind of meaningful organization is imposed on incoming material, serving the purpose of making whatever is learned more highly memorable. Greater retention will occur when the to-be-learned items are grouped in certain ways, or are classified under previously learned concepts, or are simplified in expressions as principles. For instance, the series 1 4 9 1 6 2 5 3 6 4 9 6 4 may be encoded by a rule pertaining to the squares of numbers, which can readily be seen if the numbers are grouped: 1 4 9 16 25 36 49 64 (Katona, 1940).

An example of semantic encoding comes from a study (Rohwer & Lynch, 1966) in which sixth grade children were asked to learn twenty pairs of words (like BEE–DOG, STICK–COW). The children first studied the total list and later were asked to repeat the second word when given the first. For half the children, the words were presented as part of a sentence containing a verb, as "The STICK hurts the COW." For the other half, the same words were presented as part of a conjunctive phrase, such as "the STICK or the COW." The sentence form was found to be considerably more effective as means of encoding than was the conjunctive phrase. During two test-trials, each following a study-trial, the children who studied the words in sentences recalled the second word correctly 54 percent of the time. Those children who studied the words in phrases, however, recalled correctly only 34 percent of the time. It was known from a previous investigation (Jensen & Rohwer, 1963) that single words can best be learned when embedded in a larger string of words forming a phrase or sentence. This study went on to explore the effectiveness of different kinds of syntax as encoding devices. Still other research (see, for example, Levin & Kaplan, 1972) has demonstrated that pictures suggesting visual images as means of encoding can be highly effective for learning.

The process of encoding can be influenced externally, as we have seen in the previous examples. Another experiment (Carmichael, Hogan, & Walter, 1932) showed that externally suggested encoding can also influ-

FIGURE 2.3.   Changes in the reproduction of figures when their exposure was preceded by suggested encodings. (Adapted from Carmichael, L., Hogan, H. F., & Walter, A. A. (1932). An experimental study of the effect of language on the reproduction of visually perceived form. *Journal of Psychology, 15,* 73–86.)

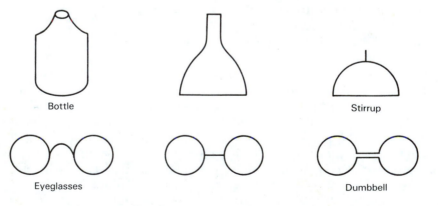

Bottle   Stirrup

Eyeglasses   Dumbbell

ence the learning of figure shapes. In this study, learners were shown twelve different figures, such as those in the center of Figure 2.3, which they were later to reproduce by drawing. Just before each figure was exposed, the experimenter said, "The next figure resembles eyeglasses" to one set of learners, whereas he said "The next figure resembles a dumbbell" to another set of learners; and so on for the remaining figures. The reproductions drawn by the learners clearly indicate the effect of these verbal communications on the encoding process.

While it is possible for encoding procedures to be suggested externally, it should be borne in mind that learners may use their own schemes, which may be quite idiosyncratic, and that these often are more effective than others that are supplied for them. In many instances of learning, encouraging learners to encode in whatever manner they choose may be the best procedure.

What implications for teaching might be suggested by this research? For example, suppose beginning readers are learning new words. What might a reading teacher do to facilitate *semantic encoding?* List your suggestions below.

Some possibilities are:
>   Present the words in sentences.
>   Have the children create their own sentences using the words.
>   Present pictures with the words.
>   Have the children draw pictures (or construct models in clay, etc.) of the words.
>   Have the children create internal images of the words or of sentences using the words.

Storage in Long-Term Memory

The learned material, transformed by the encoding process, now enters into long-term *memory storage.* The processes that occur while information is in this state are least well known, probably because they are least accessible to investigate. Here are some of the possibilities:

1. What is learned may be stored in a permanent fashion, with undiminished intensity over many years, as though it were stored on permanent magnetic tape. This possibility is suggested by neurological studies made during sur-

gical operations on the brain (Adams, 1967). When small areas of the brain surface are stimulated electrically, the patient may experience entire scenes of moments in her past life in rich detail.

2. Some kinds of things that are learned may undergo very gradual *fading* with the passage of time. This suggestion arises from the known gradual losses of memory that occur over many years in all of us. An individual may be able to recall fewer and fewer details of what he knows about a childhood friend, for example, even though the friend's name remains memorable as the years go on.

3. Memory storage may be subject to *interference,* in the sense that newer memories obscure older ones because they become confused with them (or, less probably, erase them). A newly learned telephone number, for example, may initially become confused with a number it has replaced and then apparently block it out entirely. The phenomenon of interference is well known in relation to memory. However, it is by no means certain that this effect occurs in the memory store itself—it may instead be something that happens in the retrieval phase (to be described next).

Thus, there are real limits to what is now known about memory storage and its properties. It may have the fundamental characteristic of permanence, or this property may only be partial, applying to some kinds of memories and not to others. One aspect of memory storage that should be emphasized, however, is the fact that the capacity of long-term memory is very great. There is little indication that newly learned entities take the place of previously learned things because there is "no more room." We simply do not know the full extent of this capacity. As exhibited in highly educated people, it seems virtually limitless. No one should imagine that a student's long-term memory can be overloaded.

While not much is known about long-term memory storage, we do know that it may be subject to *interference.* And there are ways of avoiding or reducing interference. Some examples are listed below.

> A teacher periodically reviews topics previously taught as new ones are introduced.

> Music students regularly practice previously learned scales as they acquire new ones.

> A religion teacher points out similarities and differences between Buddhism, studied last week, and Zen Buddhism, the current topic of study.

What other examples can you generate of ways to reduce or avoid interference?

Search and Retrieval

In order to qualify as a more-or-less permanent behavior modification, an act of learning must include the *recall* of what is learned so that it can be exhibited as a performance. The processes at work include both *search* and *retrieval*. Somehow, the memory store is searched until a familiar item is recognized, and then an entire complex of memories is revivified. What has been stored becomes accessible in working memory. The process presumably operates even on material that has been learned only a few minutes previously. However, there may be differences in retrieval strategies for recent and for longer-term memories.

As is true for most other processes of learning, the process of retrieval may be affected by external stimulation. *Cues* for retrieval may be suggested by verbal communications to the learner. For example, in jogging the memory of a student who is trying to recall what *specific gravity* means, one might say "Do you remember Archimedes?"

Sometimes, the external cue takes the form of reminding learners of their previous encoding, as in the following example (Tulving & Pearlstone, 1966). High school students were asked to learn lists of words belonging to certain categories (four-footed animals, weapons, professions, and others). The words themselves, corresponding to these categories, were terms such as cow, rat; bomb, cannon; engineer, lawyer. They were randomly arranged in lists of three different lengths, containing twelve, twenty-four, or forty-eight words. Learners were given the task of learning and remembering the words in the list. The words were read, and each was preceded by a category word, which the learners were told did not have to be remembered. Later, one group of learners recalled the words by being given cues for the categories, while another group was not given these cues. For the short lists of twelve words, providing cues made little difference in recall. For the forty-eight word lists, however, the category cues made a very large difference—on the average 74 percent (for the cued condition) to 32 percent (for those not cued). These results, then, show that previously learned categories can function as cues to the retrieval of otherwise unrelated words. Retrieval cues appear to be most effective when they are introduced at the time learning first occurs.

Again, as in the case of encoding, it must be remembered that sophisticated learners supply their own retrieval cues. As we shall see in the next chapter, an important goal of school learning is the development of independent learners. Although it is important for the design of instruction to make suitable provision for external activation of the retrieval process, it is even more important for learners to acquire strategies that enable them to do this themselves. In order to encourage such development, however, a teacher needs to know what is going on in learning, and thereby to choose judiciously the communications that are made to students.

Performance as the Result of Learning

The performance phase of learning seems fairly straightforward. The response generator (Figure 2.1) *organizes* a learner's responses and allows him to exhibit a performance that reflects what he has learned.

For the learner, the performance made possible by the act of learning serves the important function of preparing the way for *feedback*. In other words, although you may in some instances think you have learned, actually demonstrating it is the best way for you to receive assurance that learning has occurred. By this means, you obtain the satisfaction that comes from perceiving the product of learning. As a student of science who has learned how to make a graph of the growth of a plant, for example, you may proceed without hesitation to respond by constructing such a graph.

The learner's performance.   The performance of a learner has an essential function for an observer or for a teacher. This product of responding verifies that learning has taken place—that behavior has indeed been modified. The child who previously could not dependably distinguish the sounds of *a* in printed words like *mat* and *mate* now does so. The student who previously could not express 9/27 as .333 now exhibits this kind of performance unhesitatingly. The youngster who was previously unable to write a sentence using *whom* correctly now shows by her performance that she can. There is, of course, the question of how many instances of performance are required as convincing verification that learning has occurred. No simple answer can be given to this question, since it depends on the degree of generality of the performance itself. Usually, a single instance of performance is not entirely convincing; the student may have stumbled on a correct performance. If the performance is displayed in two different examples, the inference that learning has occurred is distinctly better, and three makes the conclusion quite firm. However, it may be noted that in the give-and-take of the classroom, the single instance of performance often suffices as evidence of learning.

Generalization of performance.   Retrieval of what is learned does not always occur in the same situation or within the same context that surrounded the original learning. After all, one expects students to be able to use the principle of a lever in moving heavy objects in real life, not simply in the context of a science textbook. In other words, there must be generalization of the learning that has occurred. The recall of what has been learned and its application to new and different contexts is referred to as the *transfer of learning*, often shortened to *transfer*.

A famous study of transfer was performed many years ago (Judd, 1908) and redone later by Hendrickson and Schroeder (1941). Three groups of junior high school boys, chosen to be roughly equal in age and intelligence, were given the task of hitting a target submerged 6 inches under water by shooting at it. One group simply practiced until they got three consecutive hits. A second group was given a general explanation of the *principles of refraction,* using a diagram of a rock in a lake, before they practiced. The third group received the same explanation and also a working rule, "The deeper the lake is, the farther the real rock will be from the image rock," followed by practice. Transfer of learning was assessed by the boys' performance in hitting a second target, this time at a depth of 2 inches. It was found that the third group, which had received both the explanation and the *working rule,* showed the greatest amount of transfer of learning to this second task. The working rule was apparently the most important factor in producing transfer.

We can assume that the boys who participated in this study learned how to aim at a submerged target as a result of their practice with the one 6 inches below the surface. In order to transfer this experience to the situation involving the second target, however, they needed a rule for changing aim with a change in degree of submersion. Those boys who learned about principles of refraction presumably acquired this idea in some form. It is particularly significant, though, that the group evidencing the greatest transfer learned a practical rule that could be directly applied to the new situation. Thus, this study suggests that understanding the principles in a general sense, while important to transfer, may not always be sufficient. It is likely that the working rule was more directly related to the new situation, and that it functioned as a retrieval cue to connect the principles to the new context (cf. Haselrud, 1973).

Transfer in school learning.   Since transfer is so obviously a goal of school learning, instruction needs to include the means of assuring retrieval in the greatest variety of contexts possible. *Teaching for transfer* may be interpreted as aiming to provide the learner with processes for retrieval that will apply in many kinds of practical contexts. Variety of contexts for learning thus becomes one of the important conditions supporting the transfer phase of the learning process. A further discussion of instructional techniques used to enhance transfer is contained in a later chapter.

Feedback

Once learners have exhibited the new performances made possible by learning, they at once perceive that they have achieved the anticipated goal. This *informational feedback* is what many learning theorists consider essential to the process called *reinforcement.* This process is of widespread significance to human behavior, particularly to human learning (Krasner

& Ullman, 1965; Skinner, 1968). It is important to note that, according to this conception, reinforcement works in human learning because the expectancy established at the beginning of learning is now confirmed during the feedback phase. Presumably, the process of reinforcement operates in the human being not because a reward is actually provided, but because an anticipation of reward is confirmed. The importance of expectancy to the act of learning is again reemphasized by the reinforcement process. The learning loop is closed by reinforcement. The state of expectancy established earlier makes reinforcement possible.

This feedback phase of learning may obviously be influenced by events external to the learner. Sometimes, the feedback is naturally provided by the learner's performance itself. For example, you know immediately that a basketball has successfully passed through the hoop, or the balance in a science exercise has reached equilibrium. On other occasions, you must make some verifying response to obtain suitable feedback, as when you check the "balance" of a chemical or algebraic equation. Finally, informative feedback is sometimes obtained by comparison with a standard. A child's printed *H* may be compared with a standard in a model book; the student's pronunciation of a German "ch" may be compared with feedback from the teacher or from an audio tape; your answer to an essay question on a quiz may be compared to a model answer provided in a key. The informational nature of the feedback appears to be its most critical feature, so far as the support of learning is concerned (Estes, 1972).

LEARNING IN RELATION TO INSTRUCTION

A total act of learning may be conceived as a series of events that often has as short a duration as a few seconds, or may last much longer. The phases of this series of events begin with the establishment of an expectancy and proceed through selective perception and processing in the short-term and long-term memories to retrieval, performance, and to feedback that results in reinforcement. Systematic studies of this series of events have led to the development of models of learning such as that shown in Figure 1.2. For each phase of learning, there is conceived to be one or more *internal processes* in the learner's central nervous system, which transform the information from one stage to another until the individual responds in a performance.

The internal processes of learning may be influenced by external events—stimuli from the environment, which often are verbal communications from a teacher, a textbook, or some other source. These external events, when they are planned for the purpose of supporting learning, are called by the general name of *instruction*. As the manager of instruction, it is the teacher's job to plan, design, select, and supervise the arrangement of these external events, with the aim of activating the necessary learning processes. Of course, there are instances in which few of these external influences are necessary—the learner may be self-motivated and able to carry out the various additional actions needed for self-instruction. The learners who can instruct themselves find it possible to ignore these external influences or perhaps to refer to them occasionally. Self-instruction, however, does not provide a dependable model for learning, as it is not applicable to all circumstances of school learning. Instruction is best planned so that it will always make potentially available the external stimulation needed to support the internal processes of learning.

Learning Processes and External Events

A summary of learning processes and the general nature of external events which may be brought to bear upon them is given in Table 2.1. The information in this table provides a review of the discussion in this chapter, as well as a preview of material in later chapters dealing with instructional planning.

Examples of the kinds of external events that constitute instruction are provided in the right-hand column of Table 2.1, opposite the learning processes to which they apply. For example, the table indicates that a typical way of establishing an *expectancy* is by communicating to the learner the goal (objective) to be achieved. If a designer of instruction, or a teacher, wishes to support the process of *selective perception*, one tech-

TABLE 2.1   Processes of Learning and the Influence of External Events

LEARNING PROCESS	TYPES OF EXTERNAL EVENTS WHICH MAY INFLUENCE
Expectancy	Communicating the goal to be achieved
Reception	Change in stimulation to activate attention
Selective perception	Emphasizing features of stimulus material
Short-term storage	Suggesting the activation of rehearsal and chunking
Semantic encoding	Presenting meaningful encoding techniques
Long-term storage	Not known; avoiding interference
Search/Retrieval	Presenting cues to aid search
Performance	Providing examples of performance
	Practice in a variety of contexts for transfer of learning
Feedback	Informing learner of degree of correctness of response

Below are specific examples of the types of external events teachers may bring to bear on the internal processes of learning. Match each external event with the internal process it is most likely to influence.

Internal Processes:

A. Expectancy
B. Reception
C. Selective perception
D. Short-term storage
E. Semantic encoding
F. Long-term storage
G. Search/Retrieval
H. Performance
I. Feedback

_____ 1. A music teacher presents his students with the mnemonic, *Every Good Boy Deserves Favor*, to help them learn the notes of the musical scale.

_____ 2. A biology teacher stains slides to emphasize certain features of the organism being studied.

_____ 3. Students in a math class set up a mock store and bank so that they may use their newly acquired arithmetic skills in a new situation.

_____ 4. A physics teacher suggests to her students that they keep a particular rule in mind as they attempt to solve a set of problems.

_____ 5. A master teacher reviews a videotape of an intern's first class and offers suggestions for improvement.

_____ 6. A dance instructor moves around the studio, correcting the posture of students as they perform certain dance positions.

_____ 7. A reading teacher helps a student "sound out" a word to show the student what she will be learning to read.

_____ 8. A history teacher provides certain clues to help students remember the major events that preceded the American Revolution.

_____ 9. Students learning map-reading skills are asked to locate a two-lane road, a four-lane highway, and a railroad on a regional road map.

_____ 10. A mathematics teacher has students draw Venn diagrams to help them learn certain concepts in statistics.

Answers: (1) E; (2) C; (3) H; (4) D; (5) I; (6) I; (7) A; (8) G; (9) H; and (10) E.

nique would be to provide added emphasis (by pointing, underlining, and so forth) to relevant features that serve to differentiate the stimuli being presented. If concerned with *encoding*, the instructor may suggest schemes (categorizing, imaging, linking with highly familiar scenes) that aid the encoding process, and so on. The sum total of these external events, designed to be appropriate to any given learning goal, becomes the substance of instruction.

The processes we have described, and their relationships with external events, provide us with *general* characteristics of acts of learning. Still other attributes of learning, which must be understood before successful instruction can be designed in any area of the school curriculum, are those features that are specific to different kinds of learned performances, or, to use the terms we shall employ, to different *types of learning outcomes*. This topic is discussed in the next chapter.

GENERAL REFERENCES

Bower, G. H., & Hilgard, E. R. (1981). *Theories of learning*, 5th ed. Englewood Cliffs, NJ: Prentice Hall.

Hill, W. F. (1981). *Principles of learning: A handbook of applications.* Palo Alto, CA: Mayfield.

Hulse, S. H., Egeth, H., & Deese, J. (1981). *The psychology of learning*, 5th ed. New York: McGraw-Hill.

Learning Processes

Anderson, J. R. (1985). *Cognitive psychology and its implications*, 2nd ed. San Francisco, Freeman.

Bransford, J. D. (1979). *Human cognition.* Belmont, CA: Wadsworth.

Klatzky, R. L. (1980). *Human memory: Structures and processes*, 2nd ed. San Francisco: Freeman.

Wessells, M. G. (1982). *Cognitive psychology.* New York: Harper & Row.

Learning and Instruction

Gagné, R. M., Briggs, L. J., & Wager, W. W. (1988). *Principles of instructional design*, 3rd ed. New York: Holt, Rinehart and Winston.

Reigeluth, C. M. (Ed.). (1983). *Instructional-design theories and models.* Hillsdale, NJ: Erlbaum.

THREE
THE OUTCOMES
OF LEARNING

In the previous chapter you learned that external stimulation from the environment influences internal processes within the learner to produce learning, or a change in the learner's performance. The nature of the internal processes was considered in some detail, and examples were given of external events teachers may arrange to affect these processes. Now consider how many different performances may be learned throughout people's lives. Infants learn to walk and talk, to pick up toys and clothes, to say "please" and "thank you" when they interact with others. When children enter school, they begin to learn the intellectual capabilities that will prepare them for adult life. As adults, people continually acquire knowledge and physical skills related to their jobs and personal goals.

Despite this great diversity in what may be learned, it is possible to classify performances on the basis of properties they have in common. For example, the performance of riding a bicycle is similar to that of hammering a nail in that both involve the coordinated use of muscles. In an analogous way, the performance of adding a set of numbers is similar to that of writing a grammatically correct sentence; both involve cognitive procedures in the demonstration of rules. But the features of motor skills and intellectual skills are different from one another, suggesting that the learning conditions optimal for one will be different from those optimal for the other. Classifying performances thus leads to implications that can improve the understanding of learning and provide guidelines for teaching or for designing instruction.

What kinds of learned performances are there, then? Or, in the terms we will use, what types of *learning outcomes* are there and what are their characteristic features? We now proceed to consider these questions.

TYPES OF LEARNING OUTCOMES

There are five major categories of learning outcomes (Gagné, 1972). As evidenced in the examples given previously, these categories may cut across subject-matter fields. In other words, you may learn rules in mathematics as well as in English grammar, and you may learn a physical performance in sports as well as in carpentry. But the different types of learning outcomes also occur *within* particular fields of study. So, for example, you may learn the rules for playing a game of soccer and also the physical performances required to play it. As each major category is described, we will consider examples within and across a range of subject matter, to help make clear their similarities and differences.

The five major categories of learning outcomes, in no particular order of complexity or importance, are: (1) *verbal information,* (2) *intellectual skills,* (3) *cognitive strategies,* (4) *attitudes,* and (5) *motor skills.* The following sections of this chapter describe the major characteristics of these categories, insofar as they are known at present. It will be apparent that a great deal more is known about some of the categories than about some of the others. However, the distinctions among them are adequate to make their differential properties reasonably clear.

Verbal Information

Verbal information is often referred to as *declarative knowledge,* or *knowing that.* In other words, when you say, "I know that water is composed of hydrogen and oxygen," or "I know that Springfield is the capital of Illinois," you are giving evidence of verbal information that you have acquired.

Human beings acquire large amounts of verbal information during their lifetimes. Much of such information is learned in school or other organized educational programs, but it is also acquired by word of mouth, from reading, and from radio and television. Verbal information is humanity's primary method of transmitting accumulated knowledge to successive generations—knowledge about the world and its peoples, about historical events and trends, about the culture of a civilization as represented in its literature and art, and about current and practical affairs of life.

Verbal information, then, refers to the organized bodies of knowledge that we acquire. The units of verbal information may be classified as "names," "facts," "principles," and "generalizations." In school settings, they are most often learned by being presented in textbooks or oral lectures. Sometimes, however, information may be learned by interpreting something that is seen. For example, presented with a picture, you might acquire information about it by "saying to yourself" that there are oak trees in the foreground. Regardless of how information is presented, though, it is learned by being incorporated into some more comprehensive meaningful complex already in memory. In other words, when you learn about the chemical composition of water, you add this information to what you already know about water.

UNITS

The learning of verbal information as a performance means that the learner has acquired the capability of being able to *state* in propositional form what was learned. By propositional form we mean as a sentence. In other words, learners who can repeat the words HOUSE–BOTTLE–MOUNTAIN in that order may have learned something, but they have not learned information. By contrast, learners who can state POLICE ARREST BURGLARS *have* acquired information. What makes these words information is their sentence form, which carries meaning for the learner.

To define verbal information as a statable sentence does not necessarily mean that it is stored that way in memory. Apparently, information can be stored as a visual image or as some other kind of image. In fact, the retrieval of information from memory, or "remembering," may be cued by other than verbal means. For example, a picture or diagram may serve to remind you of previously learned information. But what you are able to *do,* when you have learned information, is to *state* it, orally or in writing. Of course, this may mean stating in your own words, rather than in an exact verbatim form.

The functions of information and knowledge. Verbal information, particularly when it occurs as organized knowledge, has a number of useful functions for the student. First, it often serves as a necessary *prerequisite* for further learning. Suppose, for example, you are learning about how to predict the weather. In order to learn principles of weather forecasting, you would need information about clouds, winds, temperature ranges, terrain features, and so on. In your course on weather prediction,

Obviously, verbal information represents an accepted educational goal, and you will be learning about conditions that may be designed to support the learning of verbal information. Therefore, to help you begin to think about items of verbal information as goals for instruction, here are some specific examples.

1. Stating the requirements for achieving an A grade in a given course.
2. Reciting a Shakespeare sonnet.
3. Listing the steps for taking a blood sample.
4. Defining Piaget's stages of cognitive development.
5. Stating the rules for scoring a tennis match.

For practice, generate your own examples of verbal information in the space below.

your text, or a teacher's lesson, will likely present these necessary items of information first, before explaining how weather prediction is done. The chapter on weather prediction methods may contain an initial section that reviews previously learned information about these matters.

Some kinds of information are of practical importance to us in our lives. These include the names of common objects, the days of the week, the months of the year, and many other *labels* required for everyday communication. People retain and use information about locations, such as their city, state, country, and other countries and locations around the world. Also learned and stored is basic information pertaining to certain jobs or professions, such as teacher, lawyer, physician, and so on. The amount and kind of such practically useful information learned by different individuals depends on their inclinations. Probably you know someone who is readily able to state all the emergency phone numbers or give accurate directions to any location in your city. Obviously the school attempts to provide at least the minimum essentials of practical information for all students.

A third function of knowledge is a very important one, although how it operates is not yet well known. Organized and associated bodies of knowledge are believed to provide a *vehicle for thought*. In other words, when you attempt to solve some new problem, you "think of" many things in your search for a solution. You are not yet employing logic; that will come later. Instead, you are searching among all the various items of information available to you in memory. Using organized information, you may be able to make an analogy between some aspect of the problem you are solving and something you already know that will enable you to solve the problem. The enormous store of information which most individuals possess provides almost limitless possibilities for flexible thinking.

Intellectual Skills

A second important category of learning outcomes is *intellectual skills* (Gagné, 1985). Simply stated, these involve *knowing how,* as opposed to information in the sense of *knowing that.* In other words, when you know how to convert fractions to decimals, or how to make verbs agree with subjects of sentences, or how to identify live oaks as opposed to water oaks, you have acquired intellectual skills. Intellectual skills involve your ability to carry out these actions, not just to state them or talk about them.

It would not be possible to learn all these things as verbal information, or as facts, because too many individual instances exist. The intellectual skills you learn enable you to respond adequately to entire *classes* (that is, groups or categories) of interactions with the environment through *symbols,* such as letters, numbers, words, or diagrams.

Intellectual skills are divided into several subordinate categories, and these subcategories can be ordered according to the complexity of mental operations they imply. Furthermore, they are related to each other in that the more complex skills require the prior learning of simpler skills. The names of these intellectual skills and their ordering are shown in Figure 3.1. Beginning with the simplest, they are *discriminations, concrete concepts, defined concepts, rules,* and *higher-order rules.* (Actually there are even simpler learned entities, but we shall not be concerned with them here. See Gagné, 1985, pp. 22–45.)

Beginning with the simplest, we now take a closer look at the nature of each of these learned skills. In so doing, we will present specific examples of each in a variety of subject areas and then consider how they are related within a single subject area.

Discriminations. In responding to the environment via symbols, one of the first skills to be acquired is the ability to distinguish one feature of an object from another, which includes distinguishing one symbol from another. The infant, for example, learns gross discriminations pertaining to features of the environment—colors, shapes, and sounds—before learning to speak. As the child gains experience, these discriminations continue to increase in the fineness of detail to which they refer (Gibson, 1968). For example, the colors red and yellow might initially

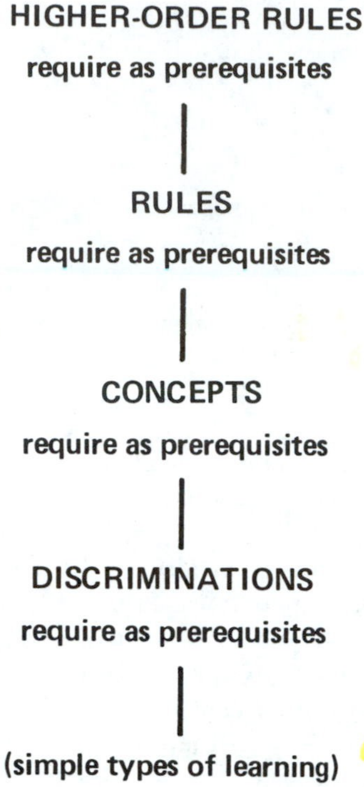

HIGHER-ORDER RULES

require as prerequisites

|

RULES

require as prerequisites

|

CONCEPTS

require as prerequisites

|

DISCRIMINATIONS

require as prerequisites

|

(simple types of learning)

FIGURE 3.1.
Varieties of intellectual skills, arranged (bottom to top) in order of increasing complexity.

provoke the same response in a child. Later, however, the child can distinguish between them and may also be able to distinguish among different shades of each.

By the time children begin to attend school, they have learned a great many important discriminations, but some have not yet been acquired. Thus, early education is often concerned with the learning of finer discriminations of shapes, textures, sounds, and other kinds of object features. Examples include learning to distinguish between the printed letter forms *m* and *n*, or between the sounds of letters such as *v* and *b*.

Discrimination learning is simply another name for the perceptual learning mentioned in the previous chapter. When completed, it results in the selective perception of features of the learner's environment. While much discrimination learning occurs in the early years of life, it is not confined to that period. For example, when learning a foreign language, you must learn to distinguish new foreign word sounds, such as the sound of the French *u*.

The performance made possible by discrimination learning is the ability to tell the difference among stimuli. This means that the learner can respond differently to different stimuli, but may not be able to name them or use them in some other way. That will come later. At an early age the child may, for example, be able to tell the difference between blocks and balls by sorting each into a separate pile. But she will not be able to name them as "blocks" or "balls" nor will she be able to respond correctly to the request, "Give me a ball." Of course, she must be able to discriminate features of objects before she can learn to name them. Thus, learning discriminations is important mainly because it is a necessary prerequisite to other learning.

Other examples of discrimination learning include:
1. Hearing a difference between two notes played on the piano.
2. Distinguishing among different colors of socks in a drawer by pulling out a matched pair.
3. Distinguishing between the symbols > and <.
4. Feeling a difference between two types of cloth.

Can you name some of your own examples?

Concrete concepts.   Once the prerequisite learning of discriminations has taken place, *concept learning* may occur. The simplest form of concepts are *concrete concepts,* which are classes of object features, objects, and events. Again, many concrete concepts are learned in early childhood, but new concepts may be learned at any time during one's life.

Once a child can distinguish *b*s from *d*s, he can learn to *identify* letters as *b*s or *d*s. Similarly, once a music student can hear a difference between two notes on a piano, she can learn to name one as higher or lower, or even to name each as a separate note.

Young children learn a number of concrete concepts identifying objects in the environment, such as chair, table, door, tree, dog, cat. They also learn object qualities, such as color, round, pointed, smooth, scratchy, and the like. Finally, some concrete concepts are relational, such as up, down, higher, lower, near, far. At school, children learn many more concrete concepts, as, of course, do individuals throughout formal schooling and at various times in their lives. You may, for example, learn the concept *marlinspike* only upon becoming a sailor or "rigger" (some-one who installs all the rigging and ropes used on sailboats).

The performance indicative of concrete concept learning is the ability to identify a class of objects, object qualities, or relations by point-ing out one or more instances of the class. This "pointing out" may be done in various ways, such as by pointing, or marking or circling with a pencil, or whatever; the means of responding is not important. What is important is that the acquisition of a concrete concept enables the learner to identify the entire class of things by indicating one or more examples of the class.

Often, identifying a concrete concept is shown by naming. For ex-ample, you might show a picture of an elephant to a child and ask, "What is this animal?" The correct response of "elephant" would be evidence to you that the child had acquired the concept.

Using the name in identifying concrete concepts, however, is not essential to learning the concepts. You may, for example, be able to iden-tify a class of object qualities, say, five-sidedness, without knowing the term *pentagon*. The converse is also obviously true—you may be able to make the verbal response "pentagon" without being able to identify any instances of pentagonal shapes. Thus, having the capability of a concrete concept means knowing the meaning of a name or label, which is to say, being able to identify the class by means of its particular instances.

Let's consider a few more examples of concrete concept learning. Remember that it involves learning to *identify* examples of objects, object qualities, or object relations. Examples include:

1. Identifying the middle of a group of objects.
2. Arranging a group of different sized straws from largest to smallest.
3. Pointing out examples of sharks among pictures of many different fish.
4. Marking all the squares on a paper showing circles, triangles, and squares.

Generate your own examples below.

Defined concepts.   Some concepts of objects, object qualities, and relations cannot be identified by pointing them out. They must instead be *defined*. Consider, for example, the concept of *obstacle*. Many kinds of things might serve as obstacles, making it impossible to identify the entire class by pointing to a few examples. Therefore, this very general class must be identified by means of a definition, such as "an obstacle is something that stands in the way." Many relational concepts must also be defined, rather than directly pointed out, as in the case of *uncle* or *buyer*. Obviously, much of what is learned in school is composed of defined concepts.

You might wonder at this point about concepts that may be pointed out directly *and* identified by means of a definition: are they concrete or defined? The answer is that concrete concepts can be replaced or given added meaning by defined concepts, and it is often the aim of education to do so. For example, young children originally learn the concepts *two* and *three* as concrete concepts. They are able to identify groups of two or three objects by pointing them out. In school, these concepts are generally replaced by defined concepts in which three, for example, becomes "a set formed by joining the set one to the set two," thus enabling the learner to use the concept in more abstract fashion. Similarly, the concretely identifiable flower becomes by definition in science class "the part of a seed plant containing the reproductive organs and their envelopes." For many purposes, of course, the concrete concept continues to be used as a means for communication: how many poets, for example, would be able to *define* a flower or would have any reason to want to?

In order for learners to show they have acquired a defined concept, they must show how to use its definition. In doing this, they classify instances of the concept. For example, suppose a ninth grade student in English has learned the concept of alliteration. She must show how to use the definition "alliteration is a poetic device in which the same consonant sound is repeated at the beginning of several words in a sentence or line of poetry." This means, of course, that she must be able to identify the component concepts, such as *consonant sound, beginning, sentence,* and so forth. Then, using the definition, she could classify examples of alliteration, such that "she sells seashells by the seashore" would be an example while "he cleverly changed the circuit" would not. (In the second example, the letter "c" is repeated but the consonant sound is not.) Note that it is not necessary for her to *state* the definition in order to show that she has learned the concept.

Rules.   A widely occurring kind of intellectual skill is called a *rule*. We often think of a rule as a verbal statement, such as "the area of a rectangle is its length times its width." But the statement of a rule is merely the representation of it—the rule itself is a learned capability of the learner. In other words, an observer knows that the learner has acquired this rule when he can use it to find areas of various rectangles, not when he can

What other examples of defined concepts you may have learned come to mind? List them below.

If your examples resemble those below, you have the idea. In fact, you have learned the defined concept of defined concept!
Classifying examples of the learning outcome of verbal information.
Classifying governments as democracies using the definition.
Identifying all the grocers described in a story using the definition.

merely repeat the verbal statement. Rules make it possible to *do* something, using symbols (most commonly, the symbols of language and mathematics). It is important to distinguish this ability of *doing* something from *stating* something, which is the verbal information outcome we discussed previously.

There are many examples of rule learning in education. When you learn to read, you begin by learning rules for *decoding* words. Similarly, you learn rules of spelling, of grammar, and of computation in arithmetic. Older students learn rules that enable them to balance chemical equations, to construct foreign language sentences, or to read music. All of these kinds of learning involve the use of symbols to represent and interact with the environment in *generalized* ways. Their learning makes it possible for a learner to exhibit rule-governed behavior.

Rules make it possible for us to respond to a *class* of things with a *class* of performances. For example, when you learn the rule for forming an adverb to modify an adjective, you know that *ly* must usually be added to the modifier, so that you would write "greatly excited" rather than "great excited." Furthermore, because you know the rule that *ly* must be added, you can apply it to an entire class of words instead of learning an adverbial form for every adjective in the language. This enables you to respond correctly to words you have never seen before. In this way, competence is enormously extended.

Higher-order rules.   After sets of simple or individual rules in a subject area are learned, they may be combined into more complex rules used in the solving of problems. A higher-order rule is still a rule and differs only in complexity from the simpler rules that compose it. This means that a higher-order rule is verified in the usual way—by noting

Remember that rules enable learners to do something, not just to state it. Therefore, when we want to see whether learners have acquired a rule, we ask them to demonstrate it, as in the examples of rules given below.

1. Demonstrating that a + b = b + a.
2. Demonstrating how to construct sentences in question form.
3. Showing that force equals mass times acceleration.
4. Finding the averages of groups of test scores.

List your own examples of rules in the space below.

that the learner can apply it to a problem at hand and perhaps to similar problems.

Consider, for example, the problem shown in Figure 3.2, which is to find the area of a four-sided figure of the dimensions indicated. In order to do this, a number of simpler rules must be applied, such as the

FIGURE 3.2. Solving the problem of finding the area of a regular four-sided figure utilizes subordinate rules and results in a higher-order rule.

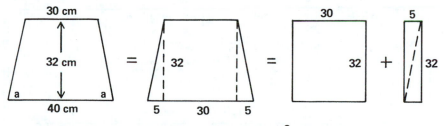

30 x 32 + 5 x 32 = 1120 cm^2

SUBORDINATE RULES

Area of rectangle
Identity of right triangles
Division of rectangle into two equal triangles by diagonal
Multiplying
Adding

HIGHER-ORDER RULE

Divide figure into rectangle and triangles; combine identical right triangles into rectangle; find areas of rectangles and add.

rule for finding the area of a rectangle, the rule for identity of right triangles, and others. Solving the problem requires putting these together to
arrive at a higher-order rule that is applicable to all such figures, whatever their dimensions. Of course, these subordinate rules are not all that
is involved in the thinking process, but they are prerequisite to attaining
the higher-order rule.

Examples of higher-order rules in mathematics tend to be neat and
unambiguous. But we presume the process of problem-solving is much
the same whatever the field of study. People solve problems, and therefore derive higher-order rules, in writing paragraphs, speaking a foreign
language, using scientific principles, and applying laws to situations of
social or economic conflict. In every case, simpler rules are combined
into the higher-order rule (or rules) that is then applied to the problem
being addressed.

Since higher-order rules are verified in the same way as rules,
learners must demonstrate in some way that they have been
acquired. Typically, this means that the learner solves problems, or
generates the rule(s) by which they may be solved. Consider the following examples:

1. Generating a rule for planning balanced budgets, given fixed income
   and fixed expenses.
2. Generating a study schedule, given class and mealtimes as well as
   time commitments.
3. Generating a lesson plan, given class objectives, activities, time, and
   resource constraints.

What examples of higher-order rules can you generate?

Summary of intellectual skills. The types of intellectual skills we
have described enable the learner to do various things by means of sym-
bolic representations of the environment. Perhaps the best general word
to describe the capabilities that intellectual skills imply is *demonstrating*.
If you have learned an intellectual skill, you can *demonstrate* its application to one or more particular instances of the class of phenomena to
which it refers.

As we have seen, intellectual skills vary in complexity from discriminations (the simplest), to concrete concepts, to defined concepts, to rules,

and finally, to higher-order rules (the most complex). They also build upon each other, in the sense that simpler ones are prerequisites for the more complex skills. This ordered character of intellectual skills has definite implications for their learning, as we shall see in the next chapter.

The prerequisite relationship among intellectual skills has been partly illustrated by the problem in Figure 3.2. There, if you recall, the higher-rules for finding the area of the four-sided figure depended on the area of a rectangle for establishing the identity of right triangles and others. To analyze the example further, we can see prerequisite concepts and discriminations upon which the rules depend. What might these be?

Prerequisite *concepts:*

Prerequisite *discriminations:*

Check your ideas with some of the possible answers listed below.

Concepts: rectangle
    triangle
    centimeter
    any of the numbers (5, 30, 32, etc.)
    the meaning of the symbols +, =, x
Discriminations: distinguishing rectangles from triangles
    distinguishing the symbols from one another
    distinguishing numbers from letters, as well as variations
    of each.

Cognitive Strategies

Cognitive strategies refer to the ways by which learners guide their attending, learning, remembering, and thinking. Our abilities to engage in these self-monitoring, self-guiding activities make possible *executive control.* (Remember from Chapter 1, Figure 1.2, that these are the processes that activate and modify other learning processes.) The nature of cognitive strategies might best be made clear by contrasting them with intellectual skills. Intellectual skills are oriented toward aspects of the environment; they enable us to deal with numbers, words, and symbols that are "out there." By contrast, cognitive strategies govern our individual ways of dealing with the environment by influencing internal processes that are "in there." Let's consider some examples.

You use a particular cognitive strategy when you attend to only some of what you are reading; what you attend to is governed by the strategy. For example, you might read only the first and last sentence in a paragraph just to get an idea of what the paragraph is about. What you actually learn from the paragraph may be verbal information or an intellectual skill, but the cognitive strategy has determined your way of learning either of these. You use particular strategies to help you learn something and other ones to help you recall it. Most importantly, you use cognitive strategies in thinking about what you have learned and in solving problems. Cognitive strategies are simply ways you have of managing the processes of learning, remembering, and thinking.

Obviously, cognitive strategies are of great importance as learning goals in education. To the extent that strategies of attending, encoding, retrieving, transfer, and problem solving can be learned and improved by formal educational means, learners will increasingly become *self-learners* and *independent thinkers*. Especially as information and technology proliferate, the goal of acquiring cognitive strategies seems increasingly worthwhile and important. Unfortunately, while "learning how to learn" and "learning how to think" are often cited as educational goals of high priority, effective instruction that supports them has been scanty. Some of the problems involved in designing instruction to support the learning of cognitive strategies are discussed in the next chapter.

Because of the inward orientation of cognitive strategies, adequately describing a performance outcome associated with them is somewhat problematic. In other words, the strategy chosen by a learner to approach any given problem is not always evident to a teacher trying to assess its acquisition. Moreover, it is difficult to specify concretely what we mean by "learning how to think." Bruner (1971) may have perhaps captured the notion best when he made the distinction between problem solving and problem finding. In problem solving, the learner is faced with a problem "out there," something presented to him for solution upon which he may bring to bear various rules. In problem finding, by contrast, the learner defines the problem himself, bringing to bear upon it not only previously acquired rules but also personal ways of thinking in order to produce an original solution. As an example, consider a student who is presented with a problem in computer programming. She may simply solve the problem by applying her knowledge of a given programming language, that is, applying previously acquired rules to generate a higher-order rule capable of solving the problem. Alternatively, she may see the problem in a different way and solve it by creating a new computer language, differing from other languages perhaps in being more efficient or easier to use. In this case, her originality of thought is an indicator of the cognitive strategies she possesses.

Other examples of performances indicative of acquired cognitive strategies are:

> Originating a new bus route around campus.
> Creating a musical score to accompany the senior class play.
> Originating a novel plan to conserve energy during peak energy consumption hours.
> Creating an efficient system for cataloging your computer disks.

What examples of cognitive strategies can you can name?

The least helpful, merely administrative

Attitudes

Attitudes represent another distinct class of learning outcomes. Many kinds of attitudes can be identified as desirable educational goals. It is hoped, for example, that children will acquire attitudes affecting their social interactions, such as tolerance for racial and ethnic differences, kindness to others, helpfulness, thoughtfulness of others' feelings. Attitudes of this sort may be initially acquired at home, or they may be promoted in social situations involving other children in the early grades of school.

A second general class of attitudes consists of positive preferences for certain kinds of activities, like listening to punk rock or classical music, playing computer games, running or strength training, or even liking to learn. A third general class of attitudes pertains to citizenship—a love of country, a concern for societal needs and goals, a willingness to undertake the responsibilities of citizenship. These three major classes merely serve to suggest the range of desirable attitudes; they do not exhaust the possibilities.

Attitudes are sometimes coupled in thought with *values*. Values are generally considered to be more general in nature, whereas attitudes are more specifically oriented toward particular preferences. Attitudes are also referred to as the *affective domain* (Krathwohl, Bloom, & Masia, 1964), a phrase which emphasizes their emotional component. While attitudes certainly involve feelings, the learning of attitudes is more than just the "training of emotions." Therefore, we will consider attitudes here in the sense that they affect human performances.

An attitude, then, is *an acquired internal state that influences the choice of personal action* toward some class of things, persons, or events (Gagné, 1985). Your attitude toward the disposal of trash, for example, will influence how you throw away soda cans, food containers, candy wrappers, and so forth. Your attitude toward rock music will affect the choices you make in buying record albums, attending concerts, and selecting radio stations. Your attitude toward learning about science will influence what books you purchase or borrow, what newspaper accounts you read, and what television programs you prefer to watch. Obviously, attitudes vary in their intensity and also in their direction—for example, you may have a positive attitude toward reading modern fiction or a negative one. Although school education is mainly concerned with establishing positive attitudes, attention is also given to certain negative ones, such as the avoidance of harmful drugs or exposure to disease.

Examples of attitudes are relatively easy to recognize and generate. Can you think of some desirable attitudes you would wish to teach? Remember to phrase them in behavioral terms, that is, in terms of what choices the student would make.

Other examples might include the following:

>   Choosing to write instructional objectives when planning a lesson.
>   Preferring to read science fiction over other types of stories.
>   Choosing to camp rather than stay in motels during a cross country trip.
>   Selecting an insurance plan that emphasizes preventive medicine.

Motor Skills

Motor skills, although not the most prominent part of educational goals, are a distinct type of learning outcome and essential to our understanding of the range of possible human performances. Motor skills are learned in connection with such common activities as driving a car, operating a computer keyboard, and playing a musical instrument. Motor skills are also involved in athletic and sports activities, as well as a number of occupations such as carpentry, auto repair, machine operation, and many others. In addition, acquiring motor skills is sometimes essential to basic subjects of the school curriculum. Young children, for example, learn to print and write letters, while older students may learn to pronounce sounds of a foreign language. At an advanced level, students often need to learn manual skills required in using laboratory or technical equipment.

The function of motor skills is to make possible the precise, smooth, and accurately timed execution of performances involving the use of muscles. For example, the activity of driving an automobile requires, at various times, the use of such motor skills as: (1) moving the car at minimal speed while turning; (2) backing at minimal speed, maintaining an angular direction; (3) following the road at driving speeds; (4) accelerating from a stop; and a number of others. Of course, many familiar activities including driving involve several kinds of capabilities, not just motor skills. Think, for example, of any sport you may wish to play. Not only must you learn the motor skills required to be successful in the sport, you must also learn *rules, strategies* of play, and *attitudes* of good sportsmanship. These outcomes may be involved even though motor skills prevail as the main objective of any particular session of learning.

Like attitudes, motor skill learning outcomes are usually easy to recognize. Name some likely goals involving motor skills if one were teaching a nonswimmer how to do the crawl.

Your answer might include:
>   Turning face out of water to breathe.
>   Floating face down.
>   Executing a scissors kick while holding onto the side of the swimming pool.
>   Executing an overhand crawl armstroke while sitting on the edge of the pool.

Summary of Learning Outcomes

We have now described the five major categories of learning outcomes—verbal information, intellectual skills, cognitive strategies, attitudes, and motor skills. These represent categories of what is learned. How they are learned is the topic of Chapter 5.

As a review exercise, match each example below to the category of learning outcome to which it belongs.

Categories of Learning Outcomes

A. Verbal information
B. Intellectual skills
   1. Discriminations
   2. Concrete concepts
   3. Defined concepts
   4. Rules
   5. Higher-order rules
C. Cognitive strategies
D. Attitudes
E. Motor skills

_____ 1. A fifth grader demonstrates he has learned to multiply single digit numbers by solving several problems of this type.

_____ 2. An Air Force recruit chooses to reenlist in the military.

_____ 3. A student is required to identify, by name, certain kitchen utensils.

_____ 4. A sixth grade student is able to recite a poem.

_____ 5. An economic expert originates a plan for reducing the budget deficit.

_____ 6. Given a list of foods from the four food groups and specifications for daily nutritional requirements, the nutrition student generates a daily meal plan.

_____ 7. "When I give the command to start, I want you to execute the proper mouth-to-mouth resuscitation procedure on the dummy model."

_____ 8. A social studies student states events that contributed to the outbreak of World War I.

_____ 9. An education student classifies examples of behavior typical of children in various stages of cognitive development.

_____10. A home economics student learns to distinguish between different textures of bread.

Answers: (1) B4; (2) D; (3) B2; (4) A; (5) C; (6) B5; (7) E; (8) A; (9) B3; and (10) B1.

TABLE 3.1   Five Major Categories of Human Capabilities Representing Learning Outcome

LEARNING OUTCOME	EXAMPLE OF HUMAN PERFORMANCE MADE POSSIBLE BY THE CAPABILITY
Verbal information	Stating the provisions of the First Amendment to the U.S. Constitution
Intellectual skill	Demonstrating how to do the following:
Discrimination	Distinguishing printed *b*s from *d*s
Concrete concept	Identifying the spatial relation "below"
Defined concept	Classifying a "city" by using a definition
Rule	Applying the rule for finding the area of a triangle to specific examples
Higher-order rule	Generating a rule for prediction of rainfall, given conditions of location and terrain
Cognitive strategy	Adopting a technique of imaging a map to recall the names of states
Attitude	Choosing swimming as a preferred exercise
Motor skill	Executing the performance of planing the edge of a board

Table 3.1 provides a review of the main points of our description of these learned human performances. Each of the five categories is listed, along with a new example of the kind of performance that can be inferred from the acquisition of the learning outcome. The subcategories of intellectual skills are separately identified with examples, since the distinctions among them, and their ordered relationships, are of importance to instruction.

Whatever their basis in internal processing and storage, these categories of learning outcomes have differing implications concerning how they might be best learned, and therefore, taught. In the next chapter, we will consider how a teacher or designer of instruction might optimally arrange conditions in order to be successful in achieving a number of different learning goals.

GENERAL REFERENCES

Varieties of Learning Outcomes

Bloom, B. S., Hastings, J. T., & Madaus, G. F. (1971). *Handbook on formative and summative evaluation of student learning.* New York: McGraw-Hill.
Gagné, R. M., Briggs, L. J., & Wager, W. W. (1988). *Principles of instructional design,* 3rd ed. New York: Holt, Rinehart and Winston.

Intellectual Skills; Verbal Information

Gagné, R. M. (1985). *The conditions of learning,* 4th ed. New York: Holt, Rinehart and Winston.

Motor Skills

Fitts, P. M., & Posner, M. I. (1967). *Human performance.* Belmont, CA: Brooks/Cole.
Singer, R. N. (1980). *Motor learning and human performance.* New York: Macmillan.

Attitudes

Mager, R. F. (1968). *Developing attitude toward learning.* Belmont, CA: Fearon.
Martin, B. L., & Briggs, L. J. (1986). *The affective and cognitive domains: Integration for instruction and research.* Englewood Cliffs, NJ: Educational Technology.
Triandis, H. G. (1971). *Attitude and attitude change.* New York: Wiley.

Cognitive Strategies

Bruner, J. S. (1971). *The relevance of education.* New York: Norton.
O'Neil, H. F., Jr. (Ed.). (1978). *Learning strategies.* New York: Academic Press.
Segal, J. W., Chipman, S. F., & Glaser, R. (Eds.). (1985). *Thinking and learning skills: Relating instruction to research,* Vol. 1. Hillsdale, NJ: Erlbaum.

FOUR
LEARNER MOTIVATION

Learning takes place in people who are motivated. It is difficult to imagine someone who is completely unmotivated; we normally think of each person as experiencing wants for something, however trivial, every minute of every day. The most fundamental motivation for a learner is the desire to *enter into a learning situation,* and we make the assumption that learners have already been motivated to place themselves in learning situations when they attend a class, view television, or read printed pages. As an act of learning continues over time, however, several factors prevail that will determine whether this motivation is sustained. These conditions, along with their sources, are the principal subject of this chapter. In practical terms, we shall be dealing here with *motivation for learning* in its various aspects.

Teachers are usually highly aware of the importance of motivation to the learning of their students. They frequently observe situations in which students' attention drifts away from assigned tasks, or occasions in which, despite prior careful lesson planning, an air of unhappiness filters into the atmosphere of the class during the lesson's activities. Experience of this general sort leaves little ground for doubt that learner motivation is an essential factor in learning. Before the stimuli within the learning situation can have their effects, and during the time they are acting upon the learner, there must be within the learner a state of motivation that relates to these stimuli. Thus, planning for the activation of an appropriate motivational state must be an early step in instructional planning. Motivation must be activated (or at least have an identified occurrence) before learning begins and during the time it is taking place. Even the events that occur *after* learning, as you will readily appreciate, have a significant effect on motivation for subsequent occasions of learning. Receiving compliments from your writing teacher regarding a composition you wrote, for example, will maintain your motivation for the next assignment better than receiving only negative comments.

SOURCES OF MOTIVATION FOR LEARNING

The motives of human beings arise from basic physiological conditions called tissue needs (hunger, sex), from the action of various physical stimuli of the environment (heat, cold, shock), and from emotionally tinged cognitive states within the person. Since the basic drives and reactions to physical stimuli are themselves modified by cognitive processes (Zimbardo, 1969), it seems appropriate to deal with human motivation as one variety of stored organized *knowledge states*. While the existence of physiological impulses within any human activity cannot be entirely ignored, so far as instruction is concerned one looks for the sources of motivation in knowledge structures that affect the pursuit of learning.

Curiosity

One rather distinctive source of learner motivation is curiosity, which appears to be aroused by stimuli that are novel, complex, or incongruous (Berlyne, 1965). When stimuli are arranged in unusual patterns, pictures are presented with incongruous features or unexpected combinations are expressed in questions, these aspects of instruction have the effect of maintaining learners' attention. When such conditions are present, curiosity may stimulate learners to try new ways of perceiving what they are looking at, and also to employ novel procedures for encoding the material being learned.

The thought occurs to some educators that if we could only capture and extend in time the natural curiosity of young children, an important source of motivation would be preserved over many years of schooling. Actually, since the environment tends to contain fewer and fewer surprises as the child grows up, it is natural that the occasions for curiosity will diminish. As a source of motivation, therefore, it is best to view curiosity as having limited, although distinctive, significance to instruction. Whenever instruction can be designed so as to make use of unusual or novel patterns of stimulation, it will doubtless make a notable occasion for calling upon curiosity as a form of motivation. However, such instructional arrangements are a long way from dependence on curiosity as a single or primary source of motivation.

Achievement

A source of strong motivation relevant to learning is the individual's desire to achieve something, to be able to accomplish something, to gain control over something by action, to produce something. The urge for achievement has been variously described. For example, White (1959) identified this source of universal positive motivation as *competence* or *effectance,* the desire that individuals have to manipulate their environment so as to bring into existence a change or a product.

The achievement motive has been extensively studied by McClelland and his associates (1953). As revealed in test situations, this type of motivation shows up in stories involving *competition with standards of excellence,* engagement in a *unique accomplishment,* and in *long-term involvement* with an achievement goal. In other words, if you were working on something unique or had been working on something for a long time, it is likely you would demonstrate a high motivation to achieve that goal. Motivation to achieve, in any or all of these senses, can be improved by specially designed training programs that lead to clarification of personal goals, perception of self-improvement, and increased assumption of responsibility for one's performance. Successful programs of improvement in such motivation have been conducted with businessmen and low-achieving students (McClelland, 1976).

As applicable to motivation for learning, the desire for achievement or competence obviously refers to people's own views of what they can accomplish through their own *performances.* The desire to begin and to continue the activities of any particular learning are perceived as means to the end of being able to do something, to do it better, and perhaps to continue doing it over a period of time. All these aims involve performance, and the abilities to carry out performances, which are seen by the student as resulting from learning. Foreseeing the outcome of learning as a performance achievement is a source of strong motivation to engage in learning.

Self-Efficacy

One important source of motivation that has received much recent attention is called *self-efficacy* (Bandura, 1977). From a variety of experiences in learning and performing, individuals develop convictions that they can successfully carry out the behavior to produce particular kinds of performance. The expectations about the efficacy of their behavior differ from expectations of their performance outcomes, as indicated in Figure 4.1. This means that you may know what behavior is expected of you to achieve an A grade (outcome expectation) but believe that you cannot successfully perform that behavior (efficacy expectation).

Learners acquire expectations about their own efficacy from several sources. Most obviously, expectations of efficacy come from the performances they themselves execute and in which they experience success. For example, once you have been successful at something, you will expect to continue to be successful. Notions of efficacy may also come from observation of human models (in the manner to be described more fully in Chapter 5). Another way such expectations are developed is by verbal persuasion, for example, by suggestion or exhortation as it might be provided by a teacher, or even by the learners themselves. Finally, there is the possibility that expectations of efficacy may be established or altered by emotional arousal, leading to a newfound determination for some accomplishment.

People's expectations of efficacy of some particular behavior affect the extent to which they will use that behavior in expending effort or overcoming obstacles. In learning situations, this means that learners who have strong expectations of efficacy of some learning technique will tend to persist in using that technique even when faced with obstacles or frustrations. If the persistence ends in success, the efficacy expectation for the use of that strategy in learning situations will increase. Learning tasks requiring much mental effort, when followed by success, will also result in strengthened expectations of efficacy.

The Concept of Mental Effort

Often, motivation for learning shows itself as a factor that enables the learner to expend *mental effort,* or provides the learner with a willing-

FIGURE 4.1. Comparison of the point of reference of efficacy expectations and outcome expectations. (From Bandura, A. (1977). Self-efficacy: Toward a unifying theory of behavioral change. *Psychological Review, 84,* 191–215. Reprinted with permission of the author and the copyright owner, American Psychological Association.)

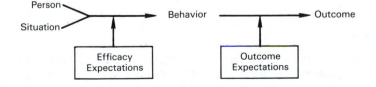

ness to use mental effort. The idea of mental effort is very different from physical effort, and the exertions required in the two cases are also quite different. Whereas physical effort can be measured in terms such as force and mass, mental effort cannot.

Mental effort is a matter of allocation of attention, as implied by the popular phrase *mental concentration.* Learning tasks are difficult to the extent that they make severe demands on attention (that is, require much concentration). The capacity limits of short-term memory serve to define the limits of the resource called attention.

A difficult task typically requires the learner to hold in mind several concepts, rules, or strategies all at once—or perhaps, to hold in mind several subsequent steps of a procedural rule while retrieving the first two steps. An example of the latter kind is remembering to use a plural verb in the second part of a sentence while still writing the first part: "People who live in glass houses seldom throw a stone, but often [amuse, amuses] the neighbors." Still another kind of task making large demands on attention is that of combining several mathematical operations (rules) in the solving of a single task, as in the well-known problem: "If a hen and a half lays an egg and a half in a day and a half, how many eggs will six hens lay in seven days?" Keeping in mind the necessity to find how many eggs one hen lays in one day requires keeping track of several mathematical rules and using them in the proper order. The task is consequently "difficult" and obviously requires careful allocation of attention.

Tasks that are perceived as difficult by learners may nevertheless be successfully achieved when tackled with suitable motivation. The mental effort required for learning can be readily put forward when motives of achievement and self-efficacy are suitably strong. With such motivation, attention will be concentrated on the difficult parts of the learning task, with the expectation of successful performance outcome.

A MODEL OF MOTIVATION

The various sources of motivation we have discussed have been integrated into a general model of motivation by Keller (1983, 1984). This conception is called the ARCS model, the basis of which is illustrated in Figure 4.2. The motives (that is, the things valued) of the individual influence the effort of learning, the expenditure of attention as mental effort. Individual skills, knowledge, and abilities determine performance, which of course is also affected by effort. Together these factors lead to consequences that are the results of performance. Two kinds of feedback from these processes are of importance (shown as dashed lines). Both effort

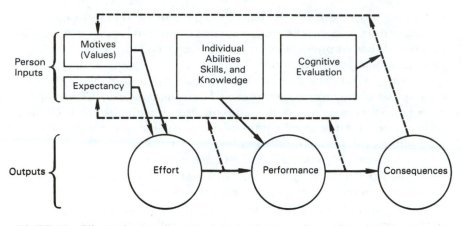

FIGURE 4.2. Effects of person inputs on behavioral outputs. Dashed lines indicate informational feedback. (Adapted from Keller, J. M., Motivational design of instruction. In C. M. Reigeluth [Ed.], *Instructional design theories and models.* Hillsdale, NJ: Erlbaum. Copyright 1983 by Lawrence Erlbaum Associates, Inc., and used with permission of author and publisher.)

and performance have modifying effects on expectancies, which in turn will affect subsequent behavior. Feedback from consequences, such as successful accomplishment, influences the individual's motives, again so as to affect behavior on the next occasion for learning.

There are four main parts to motivation, according to this model— four sets of conditions that must be met in order to have a motivated learner. The initial letters of these four conditions spell out the acronym name for the model:

A   for attention
R   for relevance
C   for confidence
S   for satisfaction.

Attention

Gaining attention of students is bound to be one of the first things an instructor does in teaching. The most general description of what is required to gain attention is the presentation of a sudden change in stimulation. An instructor may introduce such a stimulus—a clap of hands, a command in raised voice, a set of taps on a desk. Sometimes, speaking slowly or in lower tones is used as an effective kind of change to command attention. In demonstrations of objects or physical events, there are many opportunities for the introduction of sudden change.

For the establishment of motivation, however, the initial attention-getting stimulus is not enough. Attention must be maintained throughout the course of a learning act, and this requires frequent and varied presentation techniques. *Sesame Street* is an educational program whose design rests strongly upon strategies of sustaining attention. As described by Lesser (1974), the means employed to maintain attention include humor and incongruities, the encouragement of anticipation by pauses, changes of pace and style, and a diversity of characters. Specific forms of these techniques were tested during the development of this program and were adopted when found to be effective in sustaining attention.

In general, then, capturing and maintaining attention is a matter of appealing to the kinds of learner interests whose presence is known to be fairly universal—such as unexpected kinds of change, incongruous events, varied ways of delivering communications, and events that are humorous because they are unanticipated. Attention-sustaining events may be said to arouse the learner's *curiosity*, and so have the effect of making it possible for the events of instruction to begin the processing that is necessary for learning.

Relevance

A second condition for learner motivation, according to the ARCS model, is the requirement of *relevance*. This is achieved by appeal to a somewhat different kind of learner interest—the kind that convinces learners that what is to be learned will have personal significance and value for them. We emphasize that the relevance of what will be learned is as it may be perceived by the learner. What is aimed at in producing this condition may appropriately be called a learner attitude.

The simplest and most straightforward way of convincing learners of the relevance of what is to be learned is, of course, to inform them of the expected outcome of learning. Learners may be about to acquire the skills of language so that they can become persuasive speakers, or appealing writers. They may be about to learn rules of geometric shapes so that they can lay carpeting, or design shopping centers. Or, you are learning about motivation so that you may become a more effective teacher. By making learners aware of these and other possibilities, one is assuring the relevance of instruction.

The very different kinds of learning outcomes that may be seen in learners' performances mean that a single kind of relevance cannot be assumed for any group of learners. Some learners may be motivated particularly for mastery of their environment—the motive of *effectance* previously described. Others may have a greater need to interact with and influence people, and the expected outcome of instruction may therefore appeal to them in quite a different way. Planning instruction, accordingly, must be done with awareness of the differences in people that make different situations relevant to them as individuals.

Confidence

Learners need to be motivated by a belief that they will be successful in learning and in the performances that learning makes possible. This is the *confidence* factor in learner motivation. This belief in one's ability to reach a learning goal partakes both of the achievement motive and the expectation of self-efficacy, as we have described them previously.

The confidence learners have in their own abilities to accomplish certain ends varies without regard to their actual abilities. People with greater confidence tend to achieve their goals regardless of their ability level (Bandura, 1977; Jones, 1977). Presumably, confidence is built in learners when they experience success in learning on many single occasions, usually over a period of years. Youngsters in the primary grades, besides learning basic skills, may be acquiring confidence in their own ability to learn that will become a valuable asset throughout the remainder of their years of schooling. The requirement for learner confidence implies a need for careful management of occasions for success in the early years of school learning.

Satisfaction

The motive condition called *satisfaction* results from the successful completion of a learning task. In learning theory, it is *reinforcement*. The process of reinforcement takes place in learning when some expected goal is achieved and the learner is informed about such achievement. Recall that one of the processes of executive control, in the information-processing model of learning, is a set of *expectancies*. As an early event, learners acquire information about the expected outcome of the learning they are about to undertake. This information is the basis for establishment of a mental set (expectancy) of what they will be able to do when learning has been accomplished. With the completion of learning comes information (called *feedback*) of the correctness or degree of correctness of their performances. Learners see the results of their learning, or they may be told of these results in various ways. For example, your solution of an example in algebra might be reported to you as "Correct!"; or the information about incorrectness might be given in a question such as "Did you multiply both variables in the parentheses by the same quantity?"

The internal process that follows the receipt of information about correctness appears to be a matter of confirming or disconfirming the expectancy that has prevailed throughout the duration of a particular learning task. This is the process called reinforcement (Estes, 1972). Commonly, the learner experiences an emotional glow that is perhaps an integral part of the reinforcement process, although this connection has not been directly established by research. For practical purposes, however, it is convenient to conceive of reinforcement as resulting in a feeling of satisfaction, and it is thus represented in the ARCS model of learner motivation.

Summary of ARCS

In summary, the ARCS model proposes that four conditions must be met within the learner in order for motivation to be optimal for learning. These conditions are related to events that take place within the learning situation, although they may have arisen because of learner experience within similar learning situations encountered over a period of years. The provisions made for motivation within a particular learning situation may call upon motivational sources that arise from the learning history of the individual learner. Here are the conditions most important for the motivation of the learner:

1. *Attention.* Arousing and sustaining learner curiosity and interest. This is done by introducing stimulation that appeals to the learner by change, diversity, and incongruity.
2. *Relevance.* The learner is aware that the learning being undertaken has personal value or importance. Relation of the learning task to a performance outcome is shown, as is its usefulness to the learner.
3. *Confidence.* Learners must believe that they can accomplish the goal of learning successfully. A belief in self-efficacy is built up over many learning experiences that lead to success.
4. *Satisfaction.* Satisfaction is the feeling accompanying the process of reinforcement. This process occurs when the learner is given feedback information about the correctness of his performance, confirming an expectancy regarding the outcome of learning.

MOTIVATING THE LEARNER

If you comprehend the four motivational conditions of the ARCS, you will readily appreciate the states of mind of the learner that these conditions imply. There are, of course, a great many specific ways of bringing about these states by means of stimulation external to learners or of communications delivered to them. In this section we shall present a number of possible suggestions that may be used by the instructional planner or teacher to activate the conditions of motivation for learning. We shall describe some possible examples, chosen from a large and diverse set. They can be no more than examples, however, and you should easily be able to think of others that would serve the same purposes.

Techniques for Gaining and Sustaining Attention

Three categories of action can be identified as useful for arousing and maintaining the learners' attention (Keller, 1983). These are: (1) vary the appearance or sound of instructional materials; (2) use concrete examples of every abstraction that is presented; and (3) surprise the learner with novelty and incongruity.

Varying presentations of material.   When instruction is being delivered via print, the format can include variety in the form of white spaces, bold print, titles, and highlighting. When pictures or diagrams are shown on a video screen, the shots can be of short duration and changed frequently. Similarly, variety can be introduced in an audio presentation of material by a narrator or instructor. A sound track, for example, can make use of the voices of two narrators.

Using concrete examples.   General principles to be taught are often abstract. An example is a grammatical rule such as "a compound subject joined by 'and' takes a plural verb." In this rule, *compound subject* is an abstract concept, and so is *plural verb*. Examples of the first, such as horse and cow, boy and girl, house and garden, serve to make the concept clear. That is, using concrete concepts (see Chapter 3) makes the definition of *compound subject* immediately clear. The concept *plural verb* can similarly be made evident by the use of concrete examples and nonexamples.

Another way to reduce the level of abstraction is by using analogies. In explaining the working of a computer, for example, familiar objects in an office (such as files, desktop, wastebasket, inbaskets) can be used to illustrate analogous functions in computer operation. The file analogy is obvious, the desktop can represent the display surface, and the inbasket a disk to receive new files, and so on. A familiar analogy often used in science instruction is the water pipe, standing for the conductor of electric current. The physiology of body temperature maintenance is analogous to a house heating system regulated by a thermostat. By means of metaphors, the abstract and unfamiliar become concrete, and attention remains high.

Paradox and surprise.   A number of different ways are available to introduce incongruity, conflict, and surprise into the materials for instruction. A lesson on the earth's atmosphere, for example, might begin with a statement like "one of the things we breathe every day is sulfuric acid." When printed pages are being employed, striking variations in print are able to arouse and focus attention. Unusual effects may be introduced into instructional lectures by means of projected flashes of light or recorded sounds. Surprises often take the form of humor, as they do in programs like *Sesame Street,* or in the sequences of films produced by animation. Jokes, whether short or long in telling, depend for their attentional effects on the description of an unexpected or incongruous outcome—a surprise. Another strategy for maintaining attention is presenting conflicting opinions about some fact or event. This might be done by eliciting different student opinions, or by presenting contrasting opinions by knowledgeable "experts."

Other examples of gaining and sustaining student attention could include:

> Alternating lectures with discussions, film presentations, and demonstrations in a high school or college class.

> Having students think of Tinkertoy or Lego structures when teaching the structure of connecting molecules in metals.

> Having high school students debate the issues associated with legalizing certain illegal drugs in a drug education seminar.

Can you identify a technique for maintaining attention that is used extensively throughout this book? (HINT: Consider the variety of teaching interests and the diversity of persons who might be reading this book.)

In a class you might teach, what specific strategies could you employ to *vary your presentation of the material?*

... to *incorporate concrete examples?*

... to *provide paradoxes and surprise?*

Techniques for Assuring Relevance

In general, instruction is perceived as relevant by learners when they can relate what is being learned to their past experience, to something they want to accomplish in the present, and to whatever they consider worthwhile in their future. The strategies for assuring instructional *relevance* include: (1) making sure the content relates to the learner's past experience and stored knowledge; (2) explaining the present worth of the skills, knowledge, and attitudes being learned; and (3) taking steps to convince the learner of the value of what is learned for future activities that are valued.

Making the new task familiar. As an instructional planner or teacher, you will need to make an estimate of the amount and kind of knowledge possessed by the intended students. For schoolchildren, this may not be too difficult, since their previous experience with school tasks and recreations are fairly well known. In the case of adults, a much greater diversity of prior experience is to be expected, and it may be worthwhile to base the estimate on the results of a brief written survey.

The aim of this technique, in any case, is to reduce the degree of unfamiliarity and strangeness of the new learning material to be presented. For example, new concepts to be learned about the action of the heart can be related to preexisting familiarity with water pumps and valves. Algebraic operations such as the multiplication of variables in binomial expressions—for example, $a(c + x)$—are often presented so as to relate to expressions with whole numbers: $2(5 + 3)$.

Describing present worth. Relevance of instruction can often be fostered by appealing to current learner interests. The computation of an average is readily related to the sports interests of schoolchildren. Averaging can be related to game scores in such sports as basketball and baseball, or to team ratings in a variety of sports. It can be made evident to students that they themselves can find average scores and understand how ratings may be averaged. In adult classes, the effects of inflation and economic recessions can be related to financial planning for major purchases. The philosophical basis of impressionist painting can be related to personal experience in the act of seeing.

Informing about future value. In bringing about perception of the future value of instruction, the instructor or course designer here again must estimate the kinds of interests and values students have for their career and life goals. Children typically want to engage in adult activities (traveling, driving automobiles, managing money), and it is often possible to relate instructional content to such pursuits. High school students may have somewhat general career goals, such as engineering, helping people, or holding powerful positions, that can be perceived as related to particular kinds of instructional content. Adult students may have fairly specific career or professional goals (supervisory jobs, personal invest-ments, real estate appraisal, retail merchandising), and in such cases the communication of relevance of instructional content is usually fairly straightforward.

A complaint that is heard all too often among schoolchildren is, "Why should I have to learn that?! I'm never going to have to do it again after this." How might you *promote relevance* in each of the following situations?

1. A high school freshman student dislikes expository writing.
2. An inner city child sees little point in learning about the solar system.
3. A fifth grader resists reading because, "after all, in the future every-thing will be on the computer or television anyway!"
4. College science majors protest the requirement to take a literature course in the English department.

Installing Attitudes of Confidence

Learners need to feel *confident* of performing a learning task success-fully. Confidence in learning means that learners will feel responsible for their own success or failure at a task. They will believe that they can succeed in learning, regardless of failures that may occur once in a while. Such confidence is built up by experience in learning, and indeed by the kind of experience that is accompanied by success. Techniques of confidence building include: (1) communicating clear and definite learn-ing objectives, (2) sequencing successive lessons or learning tasks so that each can be readily mastered, and (3) permitting learners to take an in-creasing degree of control over the sequence of learning and over the attainment of successful outcomes.

Communicating clear learning objectives. Students like to know what they are supposed to learn, and what they will be expected to know when learning has been completed. To accomplish this purpose, clear statements should be made in language that is readily understandable, to convey the nature of the performance expected to result from learn-ing. A clear objective for the learner does not say "Study the fourth amendment to the U.S. Constitution"; it says, "What is provided by the fourth amendment to the U.S. Constitution?" A clear objective does not say "Now we are going to deal with integers"; it says, "Now we are going to learn how to add positive and negative numbers, as in finding that the sum of $+3$ and -4 is -1."

Providing the learner with a clear conception of a lesson's objective is an integral part of the procedure for learning, as will be seen in Chapter 6. The information about expected learning outcome establishes in the learner a mental set that continues for the duration of an act of learning. With continued experience, such knowledge forms the basis of learner confidence that the learning task can be done successfully.

Sequencing tasks with increasing difficulty.   When learning tasks are sequenced in such a way as to assure correct performance on each successive task, increasing learner confidence is the typical result. Intellectual skills, for example, are usually built from a progression of simpler, subordinate skills. When mastery is attained on each subordinate skill before attempting to learn the next higher skill, learning tends to proceed smoothly, and the learner's confidence increases accordingly. For example, learning to add fractional numbers is best undertaken when the subordinate skill of converting to fractions with common denominators has been mastered. This latter skill in turn may best be learned in sequence following the mastery of the subordinate skill of factoring whole numbers.

A similar set of events characterizes the learning of motor skills, when part-skills are successively put together to form the total skill. While verbal information normally possesses no such hierarchical structure, the arrangement of content having gradually increasing difficulty is a possibility that carries the same implication for the development of growing learner confidence.

Over a period of time, with successive experiences of suitably sequenced learning tasks, confidence of learners in their abilities for undertaking new learning may be expected to increase. This important attitude tends to generalize to various kinds of learning tasks in a variety of learning situations.

Providing for learner control.   When learners are given a reasonable degree of control over the events of instruction, their confidence in learning is supported and maintained. We say a reasonable degree because studies have shown that learners do not always profit from complete control over instruction. Probably the most important events for learners to control pertain to the sequence of selected learning tasks. Learners may be encouraged to control performance and feedback by selecting a new task (or a new example for practice) depending upon their own individual judgments of readiness to proceed. When done judiciously, allowing learners to judge their own degree of mastery and the likely difficulty of the task are procedures that favor the development of learner confidence.

Continued use of positive reinforcement for correct performances and achievements is, of course, a most direct way of establishing learner confidence. Over a period of time, experience with feedback for successful performances will enable individual learners to arrange occasions for reinforcement for themselves, and thus to acquire an important self-management strategy for learning.

A misconception sometimes occurs with the technique of communicating clear learning objectives. That is, if you state "You must score 90 percent on this unit to achieve an A," you may be mistakenly perceived as communicating an objective. *Don't make this mistake!* Focusing students on a grade or required score may in fact be detrimental to motivation. Instead, focus on the skill or knowledge that is to be acquired.

How might you rephrase the following objectives to communicate them more clearly?

1. Now, we're going to study different shapes that make up the world around us.
2. This class is about CPR and the Heimlich maneuver.
3. Next, we'll be looking at the interactions among various drugs.

How might strategies for instilling confidence in learners differ depending on the age and experiences of the learners? List some suggestions here:

Generating Learner Satisfaction

Actually, the establishment of *learner satisfaction* is the condition of the ARCS model perhaps easiest to arrange. In the case of each individual learning act, satisfaction is attained by using feedback to bring about reinforcement. By following this procedure over many learning occasions, the satisfaction of each single learning act develops into a self-management skill (actually, a cognitive strategy) that gives support to learner confidence, the maintenance of attention, and the relation of learning activities to long-term goals. Generating learner satisfaction includes these techniques: (1) using feedback to learner performances so as to optimize reinforcement, and (2) providing for successful generalization in a variety of contexts approximating the "real world."

Feedback to performance.   When learners have completed the learning of a single objective or a lesson, they are required to show the capability learned through performance (see Chapter 3). A learner who has completed a lesson on French definite articles is asked to use *le, la,* and *les* in phrases containing French nouns. A learner who has studied the history of World War II is asked to describe what was meant by "lend-lease." Performances are then followed by information that indicates that they have been correct, approaching correctness, or incorrect. When incorrect, it is usually valuable to include information that tells why and points to a route that would have yielded correctness. All of these are simply adaptive ways of assuring reinforcement, by acquainting the learner with the attainment of an outcome expectancy (Gagné, 1985).

As those who investigate reinforcement theory often emphasize (see Glaser, 1971), feedback is most effective when it follows closely upon the correct performance and when it is given consistently. Feedback for some learning tasks is self-evident, as is the case when the roots of algebraic equations are whole numbers. When feedback is controlled by the teacher, caution should be taken to assure that it is performance-related ("the answer is correct") and not person-related ("such a smart student").

Encouraging generalization.   Satisfaction may be broadened and deepened by assuring that reinforcement occurs not only in the initial learning situation but also in other contexts. A student who has learned about the economic depression of the 1930s can be reinforced for a successful account contrasting the events of the depression to the 1970s. The student who has learned to find the area of a rectangle can be reinforced for calculating the square yards of carpeting needed to cover the floor of a room. The student who has learned to pronounce the French *u* can receive reinforcement by reading aloud the names of a set of French streets *(rues)* with correct pronunciation.

As will be seen in Chapter 6, instruction is seldom complete until it includes provision for retaining what is learned and for transferring the learning to situations that go beyond the context of initial learning. Both retention and learning transfer require that the learned capability be exhibited and practiced in such extra-learning situations, and particularly in those resembling "real life" or the real job. But the advantages to such generalizing, besides their effect on the outcomes of learning themselves, are also to be seen in enhancement of learner satisfaction. After all, learners are bound to experience feelings of satisfaction when they are able to show that they have learned some things that are useful in the real world.

Can you think of some other examples of performance for which feedback might be self-evident? (For example, what about certain motor performances?)

How might generalization be encouraged after initial learning of the following skills?

1. Distinguishing circles from triangles from squares.

2. Learning the concept of unit pricing.

3. Throwing an underhanded softball pitch.

4. Spelling words like "receive" and "relief" ("i before e except after c").

5. Learning to construct sentences with compound subjects and predicates.

Motivation and Learning

It is often said about the conditions under which learning will take place that first you must have a motivated learner. The conditions discussed in this chapter are intended to affirm that this requirement is an important one and to show the various factors that influence its occurrence. Further than that, however, our discussion indicates that motivation is not simply a state to be attained before learning begins, but rather one to be maintained in learners during all the time they remain in the learning situation—and thereafter whenever what is learned is put to use.

The entire story of motivation for learning includes the conditions of holding learners' *attention;* convincing learners of the *relevance* of what is to be learned to both short- and long-term interests; engendering learn-ers' *confidence* in their ability to acquire new capabilities; and providing for their *satisfaction* in the completion of learning tasks and in the achievement of successful performance. These four conditions of motiva-tion are perhaps never entirely independent one from another; they in-teract with each other continually. For example, the attention that is es-tablished at the earliest stage of learning may depend in part upon a long-term interest of the learner which can be appealed to as relevant for some relatively short-term performance outcome. The sequencing of learning steps that lead to this outcome may be arranged in such a way as to increase confidence in the achievement of a performance relevant to long-term goals. And successful achievement, signaled by feedback that provides reinforcement, generates the satisfaction that will, over time, enhance both confidence and continued seeking of learning as a valued human endeavor. It may be seen, therefore, that motivation has root causes that are both external and internal. The stimulation that is used to produce attention and the informational feedback that gives rise to reinforcement are recognizable as external factors. But these produce internal states of learner interest and satisfaction that become persisting sources motivating the student to learn and to achieve.

If motivation for learning must include all four conditions—atten-tion, relevance, confidence, and satisfaction—is it possible for learners to be high on some conditions and low on others with re-gard to a particular learning task? The answer is YES! Can you think of a situation in which you thought what was to be learned was highly relevant to you but you felt very unsure about being able to learn it? Or conversely, you felt perfectly confident about learning something but it didn't hold your attention.

Since learners may vary on all four conditions, the teacher may de-cide to implement some kinds of motivational strategies and not others. For practice, describe a situation in which learners might not be wholly motivated to learn the task. List what strategies you would employ to promote their motivation and how you would spe-cifically implement those strategies in your instruction.

GENERAL REFERENCES

Motivation Theories

Bandura, A. (1977). Self-efficacy: Toward a unifying theory of behavioral change. *Psychological Review, 84,* 191–215.

McClelland, D. C. (1976). *The achieving society.* New York: Irvington.

White, R. W. (1959). Motivation reconsidered: The concept of competence. *Psychological Review, 66,* 297–323.

Motivation and Instruction

Keller, J. M. (1983). Motivational design of instruction. In C. M. Reigeluth (Ed.), *Instructional design theories and models: An overview of their current status.* Hillsdale, NJ: Erlbaum.

Lesser, G. S. (1974). *Children and television.* New York: Random House.

FIVE
CONDITIONS
FOR LEARNING

The *purpose* of learning is the establishment of internal states or capabilities. Described in Chapter 3 were the five major varieties of these learning outcomes. The *process* of learning must be supported by events occurring outside and inside the learner. In Chapter 2, you studied how support for learning could be conceptualized in a general way, that is, how events could direct attention, and so forth. In Chapter 4, events related to learner motivation were considered as they provided general support for learning.

It is still important, however, to examine how learning support may be provided to *each kind* of learning outcome. In other words, we would not expect some verbal information to be acquired in precisely the same way a motor skill is learned. Similarly, events that might promote the learning of a particular attitude could have limited usefulness for learning an intellectual skill. We must, therefore, examine the specific and unique events that facilitate learning for verbal information, for intellectual skills, for cognitive strategies, for attitudes, and for motor skills. We call these events the *conditions for learning*.

You may ask at this point, "Are there not some conditions that are essentially the same for all learning outcomes?" The answer is "yes," and some of these conditions have already been suggested in previous chapters. The point of this chapter is to give particular emphasis to those conditions that are quite dissimilar across types of learning outcomes. Then in the next chapters, both these general and specific conditions will be integrated in a theory of instruction, which can guide the activities of teachers in *planning* and *delivering* instruction.

CATEGORIZING LEARNING OUTCOMES

In using knowledge of learning for instructional planning, a first step is to identify the intended outcome or outcomes of the instruction. These *objectives* for learning may be classified into the categories of learning outcomes previously described in Chapter 3.

The performance that is implied by each learning outcome provides the best clue to its proper category. It is sometimes suggested that performance objectives be described by the use of *standard verbs* (Gagné, Briggs, & Wager, 1988), which indicate the kind of learning outcome. In fact, standard verbs are usually found to be helpful for this task of categorizing outcomes. A list of types of outcomes, the verbs used to describe their performances, and an example of each type, is given in Table 5.1.

As you may note in the table, the core of the statement describing outcome performance is the standard verb. The verb *states* means that the human capability being learned is verbal information; *demonstrates* means that a rule is being learned; *chooses* implies that the learning expected is an attitude; and so on. These exact verbs may be replaced by others that convey the same meanings; the main idea to be communicated is, What kind of human capability is to be learned?

LEARNING CONDITIONS

In a sense, learning objectives provide a view of learning "from the back end forward." As we shall see, the main reason for this view is to keep firmly in mind what the "ends" of learning are. It is time now, however, to give further consideration to the means of approaching these ends. Assuming that one knows what the ends should be, how does one get there?

In the sections that follow, we describe those conditions for learning which have been found to be of critical importance for the support of learning processes as they apply to each of the five major categories

TABLE 5.1   Learning Outcomes, Standard Verbs, and Examples of Outcome Performances

LEARNING OUTCOME, STANDARD VERB	OUTCOME PERFORMANCE
Verbal information (STATES)	In own words, *states* the provisions of the first amendment to the Constitution.
Intellectual skill	
Discrimination (DISCRIMINATES)	Given rows of printed *d*s and *b*s, *discriminates* by circling those that match a sample *b*.
Concrete concept (IDENTIFIES)	Responding to directions, *identifies* each object that is *below* another object in pictured pairs.
Defined concept (CLASSIFIES)	In an aerial photograph of terrain, *classifies* a city, using the definition of a population and transportation center.
Rule (DEMONSTRATES)	In each of several triangles, *demonstrates* the rule that the sum of angles = 180 degrees by finding the value of a third angle, given two.
Higher-order rule (GENERATES)	Given a terrain map and information about prevailing winds, *generates* predictions of relative rainfall in designated areas.
Cognitive strategy (ADOPTS)	Given the problem, "How many names of states begin with the letter M?", *adopts* the strategy of imaging regions of a U.S. map, one at a time.
Attitude (CHOOSES)	Given options for physical exercise, *chooses* swimming over other activities.
Motor skill (EXECUTES)	*Executes* the planing of an edge of a 1-inch board.

of learning outcomes. Of particular importance are those conditions that are distinctive to each particular type of outcome, or objective, and that differ as one moves from consideration of one type of objective to another. Here we are interested in describing conditions that are distinctive to each type of learning objective.

Verbal Information

What distinctive external conditions need to be arranged to bring about the learning of verbal information? What should the teacher be concerned with, as a designer and deliverer of instruction, if the student is expected to acquire information?

List the standard verbs that correspond to each of the categories of learning outcomes. Then, generate some examples in each category of verbs that convey the *same meanings* as the standard verbs.

Verbal Information:

Intellectual skills:

  Discrimination:

  Concrete concept:

  Defined concept:

  Rule:

  Higher-order rule:

Cognitive strategy:

Attitude:

Motor skill:

Why are verbs such as "know," "understand," and "appreciate" unacceptable in performance objectives?

Answers: Verbal information: *state,* recite, tell, declare
Discrimination: *discriminate,* distinguish, differentiate
Concrete concept: *identify,* name, specify, label
Defined concept: *classify,* categorize, type, sort (by definition)
Rule: *demonstrate,* show, solve (using one rule)
Higher-order rule: *generate,* develop, solve (using two or more rules)
Cognitive strategy: *adopt,* create, originate
Attitude: *choose,* prefer, elect, favor
Motor skill: *execute,* perform, carry out (also, verbs directly indicative of an action, such as "swim," "type," "lift," "swing," "throw")

Verbs such as "know" or "understand" do not indicate what capability, or performance, is to be acquired. For example, if a student "understands" democracy, does this mean the individual can *state* a definition of it, *classify* examples of democratic governments, or *generate* inferences about the lives of citizens under this type of government? The function of the standard verbs is to clearly communicate what capability is to be learned.

Draw attention to distinctive features by variations in print or speech. Imagine sitting in class listening to a lecture. How do you determine what to take notes on? What are the main points you are to learn from the lecture? Or suppose you are reading an assigned chapter in a textbook. Here again, what clues you in to important information you might be expected to learn?

Typically, important information or information that is to be learned is embedded in a context of other information, and the student's job becomes one of abstracting what should be learned from everything else. Any means of gaining the student's attention and directing it to the important information helps to ensure that the student will learn it. When information is presented orally, for example, as in the case of your class lecture, variations in the loudness or intonation of speech may be employed. Or the teacher may gain the student's attention with a phrase such as, "This is important," or with an action such as writing on the board or pointing to a diagram.

When information is presented in printed form, attention may be directed to important features by the use of variations in type, color, indentations on a page, underlining, and other elements of design. Pictures or diagrams are also sometimes employed to direct attention to distinctive features. In television presentations, repeated and rapidly shifting action sequences (as in *Sesame Street*) often prove effective in directing attention to features of letters, numerals, and words (Lesser,

1974). The main point of these techniques is that information must be perceived to be learned. What goes overlooked or unheard will not be learned.

Present information so that it can be made into chunks.   In short-term memory, no more than four or five items of information can be stored at any one time. Here the learner must contend with a limit to the capacity of short-term memory. When the verbal information is longer than this limit, as is often the case, the learner must use the techniques of *chunking* and *rehearsal* to keep the material active in short-term (working) memory. For example, during a lecture you might hear a sentence begin, "The cities in the United States with highest populations are . . ." You would doubtless find it necessary to rehearse the phrase "highest populations" while attending to the names of the cities themselves. In addition, you might employ some ways of chunking the list of cities, for example, by using LA and NY for the names of Los Angeles and New York.

The limitations of working memory play a critically important part in the design of learnable verbal information. This is the basic reason for using short sentences in printed forms of instruction. The main points of short sentences can be readily stored. In comprehending long sentences, learners must store the beginning ideas before taking in those farther on. Added rehearsal must be done, and often re-reading of the initial parts of the sentence becomes necessary. Reading is slowed up, hesitations occur, and comprehension may be diminished. Tasks of learning verbal information may nearly always be simplified by making possible the processing of short chunks.

Provide a meaningful context for effective encoding of information. Even when information has been noticed, or perceived, by a learner, it may still not be learned if it holds no meaning for the learner. For example, have you ever had a friend or teacher say to you, "Here, look at this," gesturing toward a picture, and your immediate response is, "That's fine, but what am I looking at?" Until some appropriate context is provided for the object of attention, it cannot be learned in any meaningful way. This context enhances the process of encoding and is of critical significance for the learning of verbal information.

There exists a variety of means for providing this meaningful context; what works best in a given situation depends on what sort of information is to be acquired.

1. *Meaningful encoding of names and labels.* Individual facts such as names and labels may be efficiently encoded by placing them within larger structures such as sentences. For example, the work of Rohwer

and Lynch (1966) showed that children learned word pairs such as LION-HORSE with considerably greater success when they were presented as sentences like "The LION *scares* the HORSE" than when they were presented in conjunctive phrases such as "The LION *and* the HORSE." Simple encoding devices of this sort are often useful to the human learner. For example, you might more easily learn the name of a flower like the marigold by encoding it as the sentence, "MARY's petals turn to GOLD."

2. *Mnemonics.* Another kind of meaningful context may be provided by a mnemonic (Norman, 1969). For example, the notes represented by the lines on a musical scale—E,G,B,D,F—might be remembered with the sentence, "*Every good boy deserves favor.*" Or the distinction between stalactites and stalagmites might be remembered with, "Stalactites grow from the ceiling while stalagmites grow from the ground."

3. *Advance and comparative organizers.* These are verbal passages that precede the information to be learned. They consist of verbal material which is, on the one hand, a reminder of something the learner already knows and, on the other, an organization of information to be learned. In one study, for example (Ausubel & Fitzgerald, 1961), the learners' knowledge of the main principles of Christianity was employed as an organizer for learning the principles of Buddhism. The new information was "subsumed" into a larger framework of knowledge and, at the same time, differentiated from it. The general point of the study is that individual facts and generalizations are more readily learned and retained when they are related to a more inclusive framework of meaningful knowledge, the latter being of the sort that is already available to the learner. Other kinds of organizers that can be employed in advance of the verbal material to be learned are outlines (Glynn & Divesta, 1977) and concept trees (Tessmer & Driscoll, 1986).

4. *Imagery.* Another kind of meaningful context may be encoded in terms of a visual image of a room or street; the properties of an object may be encoded in terms of a spatial "map." Instructions to use images in learning and remembering the meaning of textual passages have been found to be beneficial to retention (Kulhavy & Swenson, 1975). Often, this can best be done by suggesting the form of imagery to the learner, rather than by providing an actual picture or diagram.

5. *Keyword method.* A form of imagery that has been shown to greatly facilitate foreign language vocabulary learning is the keyword method (Pressley, Levin, & Delaney, 1982). This technique calls for the learner to associate the *sound* of a foreign word with a *visual* representation of its meaning in English. So for example, the Spanish word "carta" (which sounds like cart) may be associated with its meaning, "letter," by visualizing a shopping cart transporting a letter. The keyword method has also been shown to be effective for learning to pair proper names of well-

known individuals with their accomplishments, as well as learning to pair technical terms with their definitions (Jones & Hall, 1982).

6. *Elaboration.* Another way of bringing about effective encoding of information is by associating it with other knowledge well known to the learner. The new information to be learned can be related to some familiar and well-organized knowledge stored in the learner's long-term memory. The latter is likely to take the form of a *schema*, a kind of collected knowledge in a general category (such as "driving automobiles" or "listening to jazz"). For example, learners who heard an audio presentation of events at a baseball game related this new information to their stored schema about baseball. Those who had much knowledge of the baseball category learned and recalled considerably more of the audio passage than did those with scant knowledge of the general category (Spilich et al., 1979).

When teachers know the organized prior knowledge of students, they can suggest specific reference to a schema that relates to information to be learned. When they are uncertain about students' prior knowledge, as is often the case, they may make a more general suggestion encouraging students to relate the new information to the organized knowledge that is well known to the students individually.

Provide cues for effective recall and generalization of information. Both retrieval of information and its transfer to new situations are affected by external events that occur during the initial learning. The key point here is that recall is aided when the *cues* to retrieval are presented in association with the information to be learned (and remembered).

For example, suppose the students are now learning about the physiological effects of alcohol on the body. Later, they will be learning about, and be asked to recall, the physiological effects of other drugs. Cues may be given at the time the initial facts are presented to help students remember both sets of facts. These might include discussion of various types of effects (such as, effects on motor control, effects on the autonomic nervous system, and so forth) and how various drugs will be similar or different in the effects they produce.

Cues associated with originally learned information may also be expected to aid in the generalization of this information—that is, in its transfer to new situations of learning or use. Although the full range of future situations may be difficult to predict, transfer can be supported by providing a *variety* of contexts during initial learning. For example, the provisions of the fourth amendment of the Constitution pertaining to searches and seizures may be illustrated by concrete examples of house entry, arrest, phone tapping, and so on. These varieties of examples become the sources of later transfer of the information to new situations and to additional learning.

---

1. How might you, as a teacher, *draw attention to distinctive features* of important information in each of the examples below.
    a. In a high school history class discussing Russia's role in the second World War.
    b. In a printed lab manual for eighth grade science.
    c. In a fifth grade reading comprehension lesson.
2. How might you *provide a meaningful context,* or have students generate their own, in order to assist learning in the situations described below.
    a. Students are trying to remember the equivalent, in pounds, of 1 kilogram. (1 kg = 2.2 lbs)
    b. Students are required to learn the order of the planets in increasing distance from the sun.
    c. Learners are studying the courting and marriage customs of some American Indian tribes.

Intellectual Skills

As is true in the learning of verbal information, external events may influence internal processes of learning intellectual skills. Some of the ways of influence are similar, some different.

Call attention to distinctive features.   The communication of the skill and its procedures need to be presented in ways that highlight features of the concept or rule. If the concept *cylinder* is being taught to children, the features of circular base and straight parallel sides would be prominently displayed. If a rule such as "i before e except after c" is to be learned, words such as *believe* and *receive* could be displayed with the *i* and the *e* in bold print.

Stay within the capacity limits of working memory.   The steps of lengthy procedures, such as those involved in long division, can easily exceed the capacity of the working memory if presented in an uninterrupted sequence. To stay within these limits, such procedures are typically presented in chunks, perhaps two steps at a time, along with a hand-written array of numbers as an external prompt. Of course, the use of the hand calculator for division eliminates the strain of holding procedural steps in working memory. Other examples of capacity limits of the working memory are found in the skills of reading and writing (cf. E. Gagné, 1985). In general, tasks for learning of such skills should also be designed to stay within the limits of capacity of the short-term memory.

   Stimulate the recall of previously learned component skills.   Any intellectual skill may be analyzed and broken down into the simpler skills that must be combined to bring about its learning. These simpler skills, or "essential prerequisites," may themselves be analyzed to reveal the even simpler skills of which they are composed (Gagné, 1985, pp. 127–135). This process of analysis results in what is called a *learning hierarchy,* or a chart of the subordinate skills related to some complex skill. An example of a learning hierarchy is given in Figure 5.1.

   In order for the complex skill to be learned, the simple skills to be combined must be *retrieved* to working memory (that is, short-term memory). Learning how to calculate an average score, for example, requires that students recall how to count, add, and divide. In this very simple example, retrieval of these skills may be achieved by a communication to the learner such as, "You remember how to add and how to divide num-

FIGURE 5.1.   A learning hierarchy showing the analysis of an intellectual skill to be learned and its prerequisite skills. (From Gagné, R. M., *The Conditions of Learning,* 4th ed. Copyright Holt, Rinehart and Winston, Inc., 1985. Reprinted by permission of the copyright owner.)

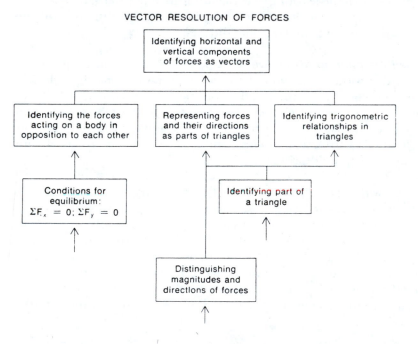

bers." For more difficult and complex skills, it may be necessary for the learners to carry out tasks involving the component skills to show that they can actually do them.

Present verbal cues to the ordering of component skills.   Once the appropriate component skills have been retrieved, cues to their combination or proper sequence must be provided. This provision of cues typically takes the form of a verbal statement such as, "First you add up all the scores; then you count the number of scores; and finally, you divide the sum of scores by the number of scores to obtain the average." The extent to which external cueing is necessary varies with the complexity of the skill to be learned and also with the learner. Some learners may be able to provide appropriate cues to themselves or may require only a simple "hint." When cues are omitted altogether, the method is called "discovery learning" (Shulman & Keislar, 1966).

Schedule occasions for practice and spaced review.   Although intellectual skills such as rules and concepts may be rapidly learned, the process of retrieval sometimes presents difficulties. Faced with a problem involving a previously learned rule or concept being applied in a new context, a learner might feel, I know *how* to do this, but I have forgotten *what* it is. Retrieval of fully learned intellectual skills may turn out to be relatively poor, even a few days following their learning.

Sometimes, a verbal cue may serve to "jog" a student's memory, bringing to mind the set of cues that will enable the reinstatement of a skill. Suppose, for example, the rule for converting readings of Fahrenheit temperature to the Celsius scale had been learned but momentarily forgotten. Providing verbal cues such as "5/9" or "-32" might be enough for the learner to retrieve the rule.

To ensure the retention of many intellectual skills, however, it is desirable to provide *practice* or *reviews*, typically *spaced* over days or weeks of time. Practice has been shown to increase the speed and efficiency with which learners can retrieve, and subsequently apply, intellectual skills. You can imagine how much better at solving certain kinds of problems you would become with continued practice doing it, or how "rusty" you might feel if you had not seen a problem of that type for some time. It has also been shown that retention of intellectual skills is enhanced when practice or review occurs over a period of time rather than massed all at once (cf. Reynolds & Glaser, 1964).

Finally, the importance of practicing certain basic skills to the point they become *automatic* has recently been reemphasized. In reading, for example, the skill of decoding words should be so automatic that learners can concentrate their attention on comprehending the meaning of what they read (LaBerge & Samuels, 1974). Similarly, the rules of arithmetic operations (such as factoring numbers, dividing fractions) should be practiced to the point of automaticity so that the learner has attention available to devote to the solving of complex numerical and word problems (Gagné, 1983). It is possible to speculate that automatization of basic skills (not simply mastery) would be a desirable objective of education in the primary grades (cf. Bloom, 1986). It is also likely that the computer, through drill and practice programs, will contribute significantly to the realization of this objective.

Use a variety of contexts to promote transfer.   Intellectual skills are important components in the transfer of learning. It is common to distinguish two kinds of transfer in which such skills are involved. In *vertical transfer,* intellectual skills exhibit transfer to higher-level skills, that is, to skills that are more complex (Gagné, 1985). The skill of multiplying whole numbers, for example, is a part of the more complex skills of dividing, adding, and multiplying fractions. Transfer to the learning of these more complex skills is dependent primarily on the *prior learning* of the simpler skills. Once the basic skills are mastered—that is, they are automatic or at least readily retrievable—they may form the basis for learning the more complex skill. This principle is illustrated by the learning hierarchy (refer back to Figure 5.1).

The second kind of transfer is called *lateral transfer.* This refers to the generalization of what is learned to new situations, differing from those in which learning has occurred. Most school learning involves transfer of this type. In other words, it is hoped that individuals will be able to take those skills they learned in school and use them appropriately outside of school. A typical example of this can be seen in the learning of simple arithmetic skills. Students solve problems in school involving the rules of addition, subtraction, and so forth. As adults, they are expected to use these same skills to balance a checkbook, calculate unit prices in the grocery store, and determine the amount of a tip for a restaurant meal.

The transfer of intellectual skills to new situations is a process that is also subject to the influence of external events in the learner's environment. While it involves retrieval of learned skills, it also requires the use of additional cues to relate the skills to the new situation. As such, it appears to be advantageous to have learners practice the application of the skill to a *variety* of situations or problem contexts. For example, once you had learned the behavior management procedure of "positive reinforcement," you would be better able to use it appropriately in your own teaching if, in class, you had identified its use in many different examples.

List *at least one* learning condition that would be important in teaching each of the following intellectual skills.

1. the concept "donkey"
2. the rule for finding the area of a rectangle (area = length times width)
3. the distinction between "p" and "q"
4. the concept "circulation"
5. the rules for generating a balanced diet

Cognitive Strategies

In considering the third major type of learning outcome, we find a different set of external influences that can be brought to bear upon the processes of learning. Since cognitive strategies are internally organized control processes, the effect of external conditions on their learning is found to be less direct than is the case with verbal information and intellectual skills. Nonetheless, there are a few general conditions thought to be essential for the learning of cognitive strategies.

Describe or demonstrate the strategy. Cognitive strategies that are relevant to particular intellectual tasks (sometimes called *task strategies*) may be easy for learners to understand and use. Accordingly, some of the simpler strategies can apparently be established by direct instruction. Rohwer (1974) has reviewed a number of studies concerned with the use of *elaboration strategies* in the learning of associations of word-pairs such as those described in the previous section on learning verbal information. Young children (ages 6 to 11) learn and remember word-pairs most readily when sentences or pictures showing an association between the words are explicitly shown. Older learners, however, sometimes acquire and recall the word-pairs more readily when they are told to supply the sentences or the mental picture themselves. Such results imply that the older learners have available effective task strategies to call upon and use, whereas younger learners do not, but can quickly acquire them when they are described.

Cognitive strategies that are more general in their control of intellectual processes have been called *executive* or *metacognitive strategies*. Quite a variety of executive strategies have been investigated as candidates for learning (Derry & Murphy, 1986). There are strategies for understanding and using text information, including paraphrasing, imagery, and key idea analysis. There are strategies that are more general in their effects, such as goal-setting, concentration management, and self-monitoring. And there are executive strategies of problem solving and critical thinking.

The strategies that govern the individual's own behavior in learning and thinking are not learned on single occasions, as may be the case with intellectual skills. Instead, they undergo refinement over long periods of time. It is this characteristic that makes them appear to be described more appropriately as *developed* rather than *learned.* The extent to which inherent growth of the central nervous system determines the rate of such development has not been determined. The theory of Piaget (Flavell, 1963) proposes that there are stages of growth that set limits to cognitive strategy development at a range of age levels: the sensorimotor period (0–2 years), the preoperational period (2–7 years), the period of concrete operations (7–11 years), and the period of formal operations (11 years to adult). Despite such limits, if indeed they do exist, it is apparent that learning plays an important role in the development of cognitive strategies.

Procedures for teaching cognitive strategies of problem solving have usually combined the presentation of verbal descriptions of the strategy with practice in solving a variety of problems. Such a method is used, for example, in the *Productive Thinking Program* (Covington, Crutchfield, Davies, & Olton, 1972). Children are given a set of booklets providing "guided practice" in problem solving. Each booklet describes a detective-type mystery problem for the child to solve. As the story unfolds, printed verbal instructions describe certain strategies to the student, introduced one at a time. Examples of the strategies included are: (1) how to generate many ideas; (2) how to evaluate the relevance of ideas to facts; (3) how to look at a problem in new ways; (4) how to ask relevant questions; (5) how to become sensitive to useful clues; (6) how to clarify the essentials of the problem. The student practices such skills in connection with each problem, and writes down ideas, questions, or suggestions for what should be done next. Results of studies using this method have shown substantial improvements in the problem-solving performances of fourth and fifth grade children, when tested on a set of entirely new problems of varied content.

Direct verbal description of cognitive strategies may thus be an effective way of arranging suitable conditions for learning them. Such communications may be quite effective in bringing about acquisition of the simpler *task strategies.* Even in the case of *executive strategies* such as those involved in problem solving, verbal descriptions (such as "break the problem down into parts," or "analyze the ends to reveal the means") may indicate procedures whose content is simple. Following such instructions, however, the learner must be given opportunities to employ the strategies, and perhaps refine them, by meeting a variety of problem-solving situations.

Provide opportunities for strategy practice.   Providing frequent opportunities for the practice of cognitive strategies is a second critical condition for their acquisition. This is especially important when one considers that the desired performance outcome of learning a strategy is original or creative behavior. Only when learners have been challenged with many novel problems can they extend their strategy use to new realms and exhibit originality of thinking. For example, a student who had never before encountered problems of urban transport would be unlikely to design a new, more efficient routing system for buses in a traffic-congested city. However, we might reasonably expect a library science student, who had dealt with a great many problems of data and resource management, to create a new, computer-based system for cataloging a library's rare books collection.

Provide informative feedback on strategy use.   Finally, providing feedback during learning is an important condition in the learning of cognitive strategies. The reinforcing events provided to the learner must be *informative* about what has actually been accomplished. In other words, if learners have been challenged to be original, or inventive, in the execution of a performance involving a cognitive strategy, the feedback should indicate the nature and amount of originality, creativeness, or inventiveness. Thus, the setting of a problem situation, or successive problem situations, is no more than half the battle, so far as arranging suitable learning conditions is concerned. The other half, equally important, is the condition of feedback, in which learners have their originality (or whatever) confirmed.

Attitudes

As we have seen in Chapter 3, an attitude is a learned capability that affects the learner's choice of personal action. Thus, an attitude is an internal state that originates processes of *executive control* (see Chapter 1, Figure 1.2).

Attitudes may be learned in a "direct" manner, or in ways that are "indirect." When directly acquired, attitudes may result from the experience of success on the part of the learner. For example, suppose you had successfully performed in an amateur theatrical effort and received much praise for your part. You would be likely, as a result of this experience, to acquire a positive attitude toward acting as a personal activity. Similarly, someone who has experienced success in painting is likely to

In each of the following examples, the goal is for students to adopt and use a cognitive strategy, or in some way to exhibit creative behavior that is indicative of their unconscious use of cognitive strategies. For each example, list *at least one* learning condition that promotes accomplishment of the goal.

1. In a creative writing class, students are to write a brief, fictional essay.

2. For a science project, students must define a problem and set up an experiment to investigate it.

3. In a dance class, students are given an emotion and asked to create a dance that expresses it.

4. In a civics class, students work collectively on the goal of increasing the number of students who vote in school elections.

choose it as a leisure-time pursuit. On another level, students tend to like those school subjects in which they have been successful and received reinforcement for that success.

Attitudes may also be acquired indirectly, and the principal indirect method of establishing and modifying attitudes is by human modeling (Bandura, 1969). Learners tend to want to "be like" those they respect or "identify with." They are likely to make choices of personal action similar to those made by their heroes or models. Can you remember an action you have chosen because someone you admire was doing it?

Whether direct or indirect methods are involved in the acquisition or modification of attitudes, certain critical features common to both must be present. Again, these are quite distinct from those applicable to other kinds of learning outcomes.

Establish an expectancy of success associated with the desired attitude.   The establishment of an expectancy is a particularly critical feature in the learning of an attitude. If the learner had experienced success following a choice of personal action, a reminder may be sufficient to activate the expectancy. For example, suppose an individual has chosen to attend a concert of classical music and has participated in the enjoyment and public appreciation of the performance. A simple reminder of this success may activate the expectancy, which is the first step in acquiring a positive attitude towards such participation.

When a human model is part of the motivating situation, as opposed to personal experience of the learner, identification with the model must be assured. In other words, the model should be someone the learner admires or respects. Then the expectancy that is established is presumably one of "becoming like" the admired person.

Provide for the choice associated with the attitude to be performed. Executing the performance resulting from the choice of action is an essential part of learning an attitude. In other words, the learner must actually do that which results from having the desired attitude. For example, if you are to learn to like reading modern fiction, then you must actually read some works of modern fiction (with suitable feedback confirming your expectancy of enjoyment).

When human modeling is employed, the model makes the choice and displays the action to the learner, rather than the learner performing the action. What is important in such cases is that the model's behavior be shown or sufficiently described. A typical example might be Smokey the Bear putting out a burning match to promote an attitude concerning the prevention of forest fires.

Give feedback for successful performance. As our previous discussion has implied, reinforcement is critically important in the establishment or modification of an attitude. The expectancy that is activated must be confirmed in order to complete the act of learning. Success following the choice of personal action may be directly experienced by the learner, as when you choose tennis as an activity and find you can score points on your first serve most of the time. When the choice of action is observed in a human model, the confirmation takes the form of "vicarious reinforcement" (Bandura, 1971). The learner must observe the model being rewarded, or attaining satisfaction from achieving the goal, following the model's choice of action. Thus, in the case of a respected sports figure rejecting an offer of illicit drugs, the consequences of this action, such as winning a race in the high hurdles, must be displayed to the learner.

Motor Skills

We come now to the fifth and final major type of learning outcome, the motor skill. Here again, certain external events have a particularly critical influence on the internal processes of learning. To begin with, motor skills involve the learning of an *executive subroutine* (Fitts & Posner, 1967), which governs the number and sequence of actions that make up the performance. This is actually a rule for procedure. In learning to print the letter *E*, for example, the child must learn to make four distinct

> For each of the following scenarios, suggest what learning conditions the teacher might employ to facilitate students' acquisition of the desired attitude.
>
> 1. A kindergarten teacher faces a particularly unruly group of children. She wants them to learn to be polite to one another.
> 2. A high school chemistry teacher is concerned about safety in the chemistry labs. She wants students to follow the safety procedures that are posted in the labs and included in their lab manuals.
> 3. A sixth grade reading teacher wishes students would share his love of reading, especially classic literature, but they seem to spend their free time playing video games.
> 4. A physical education teacher wishes to establish in students a positive attitude toward lifelong fitness.

strokes and adopt a particular order for those strokes. The learning of this or any procedure may be best facilitated by a verbal communication.

Present verbal or other guidance to cue the executive subroutine. To cue the procedure in our previous example, the teacher might say to the child, "First make a line downward, then three lines across." Examples of other motor skills whose procedures are easily cued by verbal instructions include operating a coin telephone ("First lift the receiver, then put in your coin and dial the number") and assembling a simple Tinkertoy ("Put the long rods into the holes on the round pieces").

To cue the executive subroutines of more complex motor skills may require a visual demonstration, which could be provided by the teacher, by a series of pictures or diagrams, or by a film or other audiovisual presentation. With complex skills, it may also be desirable to break the procedure into parts, each of which is demonstrated separately as well as in the entire routine. You can imagine, for example, how much easier it is to learn a swimming skill such as the breaststroke when its component parts are demonstrated and practiced than if it were to be demonstrated only in its entirety.

Besides the rule-governed procedure, the accuracy and smoothness of performance constitute essential characteristics of the learned motor skill. These are influenced by feedback from muscular movement, which means they may be indirectly affected by the external event of *practice,* that is, repeated attempts by the learner to achieve the desired performance.

Arrange repeated practice. Certainly you have all heard the old axiom, "Practice makes perfect!" In the case of motor skill learning, repeated efforts to produce the desired skill enable learners to improve both the accuracy and the smoothness with which they are able to execute the performance. In the case of printing *E*s, the child may spend considerable time printing *E*s that progressively resemble the shape of the printed model. In the case of a more complex skill like executing a lay-up shot in basketball, the player who practices eventually performs the skill with ease and lands more and more baskets.

Furnish immediate feedback as to the accuracy of performance. As in the case of other learning outcomes, the expectancy that initiated the learning of the skill needs to be confirmed. There is some evidence to indicate that the *immediacy* of reinforcement may be important in facilitating the learning of motor skills. Without immediate feedback, it is possible and likely that learners may develop "bad habits," which may interfere with their ability to perform the skill well. For some motor skills, it is not always easy to arrange feedback without delay. For example, typing students are not usually aware of having made an error in striking a letter until they check over a page containing many lines of their work. This situation contrasts with that of a skill like throwing darts, where the accuracy of the throw is almost immediately made apparent by the position of the dart on the board. Generally speaking, the evidence shows that feedback given immediately following the performance is an aid to learning (Merrill, 1971).

Besides immediacy, the *informative accuracy* of feedback has been found to affect positively the learning of motor skills (Fitts & Posner, 1967). In other words, learning processes are more likely to be supported when learners are told how close they come to a target performance, as opposed to being told simply, "You're doing well." In addition, learning may be aided by providing a standard with which learners can compare their own performance, as in the case of printing letters.

Encourage the use of mental practice. Research on motor skill learning has provided evidence for using mental practice, a form of imagery, to help facilitate the learning of complex motor performances (Lindahl, 1945). It appears that when athletes image their entire performance, their muscles respond almost as if they were actually practicing the performance. These muscular responses, however small, appear to have a facilitative effect on later performance. This technique of mental practice has seen application particularly in individual sports, such as skating and skiing, and many competitors report using it to advantage (Singer, 1980).

List *at least one* learning condition that would be important in teaching each of the following motor skills.

1. Teaching young learners how to do a forward roll.

2. Teaching education students to operate a filmstrip projector.

3. Teaching middle school children to throw a softball overhand.

4. Teaching high school students a swimming stroke such as the crawl.

LEARNING CONDITIONS IN INSTRUCTION

The processes of learning, remembering, and transfer that take place within the learner can be influenced by external events in the learner's environment. Each process of learning, as described in Chapter 2, is potentially subject to the influence of externally generated stimulation. The degree to which such influence may be applied, however, and the extent of the influence, depends upon *what is being learned.* In Chapter 3 we distinguished five major classes of learning outcomes—verbal information, intellectual skills, cognitive strategies, attitudes, and motor skills. And in this chapter, we have described for each outcome the external events that appear to be involved critically in the support of its learning. Table 5.2 on the next page summarizes the critical conditions for learning we have mentioned.

Now that we have examined potential external influences on learning processes and potential external influences critical to the learning of various outcomes, we have the building blocks for *instruction.* Instruction is the activity of planning and executing external events to support learning processes aimed at particular types of learning outcomes. It is to planning instruction that we now turn in Chapter 6.

TABLE 5.2   A Summary of External Conditions Which Can Critically Influence the Learning of the Five Major Varieties of Learning Outcomes

TYPES OF LEARNING OUTCOME	CRITICAL LEARNING CONDITIONS
Verbal Information	1. Draw attention to distinctive features by variations in print or speech. 2. Present information so that it can be made into chunks. 3. Provide a meaningful context for effective encoding of information. 4. Provide cues for effective recall and generalization of information.
Intellectual Skills	1. Call attention to distinctive features. 2. Stay within the capacity limits of working memory. 3. Stimulate the recall of previously learned component skills. 4. Present verbal cues to the ordering or combination of component skills. 5. Schedule occasions for practice and spaced review. 6. Use a variety of contexts to promote transfer.
Cognitive Strategies	1. Describe or demonstrate the strategy. 2. Provide a variety of occasions for practice using the strategy. 3. Provide informative feedback as to the creativity or originality of the strategy or outcome.
Attitudes	1. Establish an expectancy of success associated with the desired attitude 2. Assure student identification with an admired human model. 3. Arrange for communication or demonstration of choice of personal action. 4. Give feedback for successful performance; or allow observation of feedback in the human model.
Motor Skills	1. Present verbal or other guidance to cue the executive subroutine. 2. Arrange repeated practice. 3. Furnish immediate feedback as to the accuracy of performance. 4. Encourage the use of mental practice.

Summary Exercise

For each of the following examples, indicate (a) which one of the five types of learning outcomes is being fostered, *and* (b) what learning condition is being employed to aid the learning of the outcome.

Example: A music teacher tells students to think of a "face" to help them learn the musical notes corresponding to the spaces on the scale (*FACE*).
(a) outcome—verbal information (i.e., the notes corresponding to the spaces on the musical scale)
(b) learning condition—providing a meaningful context (i.e., a mnemonic device)

1. An ex–football player speaks to a high school class about the dangers of using cocaine.
   (a)
   (b)

2. "Before we learn how to write an entire essay, do you know what a topic sentence is? Let's review it."
   (a)
   (b)

3. As soon as a factory trainee on the auto assembly line assembles a steering wheel, the foreman examines it and shows her what she did wrong.
   (a)
   (b)

4. A student in a research class is required each week to write a brief summary of a study he has read. After several weeks, he develops a standard outline that he can use to make his assignment easier.
   (a)
   (b)

5. An English teacher, in a lesson on poetic devices, provides examples of the concept of alliteration as it has been used in nursery rhymes, jingles, and political slogans, as well as classical poetry.
   (a)
   (b)

6. A social studies teacher, beginning a discussion on reasons why rice is so widely grown in India, describes the cultivation of rice in the southern United States.
   (a)
   (b)

Answers:
(1) Attitude, using a role model to establish an expectancy regarding the attitude
(2) Intellectual skill, stimulating recall of a previously learned component skill
(3) Motor skill, providing feedback as to the accuracy of performance
(4) Cognitive strategy, having multiple opportunities to use a strategy
(5) Intellectual skill, providing a variety of examples to promote transfer
(6) Verbal information, providing a meaningful context (in this case, a comparative organizer)

GENERAL REFERENCES

Instructional Objectives

Briggs, L. J., & Wager, W. (1981). *Handbook of procedures for the design of instruction.* Englewood Cliffs, NJ: Educational Technology.
Mager, R. F. (1975). *Preparing objectives for instruction,* 2nd ed. Belmont, CA: Fearon.
Popham, W. J., & Baker, E. L. (1970). *Establishing instructional goals.* Englewood Cliffs, NJ: Prentice Hall.

Conditions for Learning

Bandura, A. (1977). *Social learning theory.* Englewood Cliffs, NJ: Prentice Hall.
Bloom, B. S. (1971). Learning for mastery. In B. S. Bloom, J. T. Hastings, & G. F. Madaus (Eds.), *Handbook on formative and summative evaluation of student learning,* 4th ed. New York: McGraw-Hill.
Gagné, R. M. (1985). *The conditions of learning,* 4th ed. New York: Holt, Rinehart and Winston.
Merrill, M. D. (1983). Component display theory. In C. M. Reigeluth (Ed.), *Instructional design theories and models.* Hillsdale, NJ: Erlbaum.

Learning and Instruction

Briggs, L. J. (Ed.). (1977). *Instructional design: Principles and applications.* Englewood Cliffs, NJ: Educational Technology.
Gagné, E. D. (1985). *The cognitive psychology of school learning.* Boston: Little, Brown.
Gagné, R. M., Briggs, L. J., & Wager, W. W. (1988). *Principles of instructional design,* 3rd ed. New York: Holt, Rinehart & Winston.

SIX
PLANNING INSTRUCTION

Teachers have many things to do, and one of their most important activities is making sure that the learning of students is supported in every possible way. The previous chapters have described the nature of learning processes and learning outcomes and thus have indicated the *potential* ways in which student learning can be influenced. In this chapter and the next, we propose to discuss how procedures of *instruction* can be devised and used to make these potential influences become actualities.

Two Aspects of Instruction

Like many complex human activities, instruction has two parts to its accomplishment. Because it is complex and subject to the various constraints of specific situations, it must first be *planned.* Teachers may plan specific "next assignments" for particular students. They may plan lessons for groups or classes of children. They frequently plan a set of topics to be included as part of a year or semester course and often the course as a whole. Sometimes, too, they plan larger programs or "curricula," either independently or as members of a team. Again, as team members, they may be called upon to plan an educational program for an entire school or school system, such as a program of independent study or of environmental education.

The second component, following the planning, is the conduct of instructional operations, or the *delivery* of instruction. Here the teacher may be arranging an external supporting situation for an individual student, a small face-to-face group, or a larger group like a class. Teachers may be engaged in motivating, stimulating recall, or in any of the other kinds of learning–support activities implied by Chapter 5. They may be communicating to students verbally, demonstrating how to do something, displaying some phenomenon before a class, or behaving as human models in adjudicating disputes. Thus, besides the planning the teacher has done in preparation for instruction, many moment-to-moment decisions are required for instructional delivery.

The planning of instruction will be dealt with in this chapter, leaving the matter of delivery to Chapter 8. We will describe first the basis for planning large units of instruction like courses and topics and then proceed to the individual lesson and its component events. In connection with individual lesson planning, we shall need to pay particular attention to those instructional events that are of critical relevance to the different kinds of learning outcomes described in Chapter 5. Throughout these descriptions, we continue to have in mind the question, "How can instruction be planned to support the processes of learning most effectively?"

THE PLANNING OF COURSES

Instructional planning is frequently done in terms of relatively large units such as *courses*. Naturally, such a unit of instruction may occupy various periods of time, from a few days to many months, and a definition of "course" in terms of such time intervals is not a matter of concern here. A course is often conceived as containing several *topics*, each of which in turn may have a number of different instructional objectives. Thus, a course in American government might include topics on local government, state government, the Congress, the court system, and so on. Each topic in its turn may be further subdivided into subtopics and then into lessons.

Teachers sometimes plan courses based on a structure provided by a textbook or other curricular materials. Within these frameworks, teachers may make a variety of adaptations to insure the best usage of the course materials. In other cases, teachers or teams of teachers may undertake to plan a series of topics or an entire course, which will entail developing new materials. Here we shall describe course planning without regard to the question of whether the materials are being designed initially or whether they are selected from existing texts and adapted for class-room use.

The rules of planning applicable to courses and topics are primarily the rules of outlining. In other words, more inclusive entities are broken down into logically subordinate ones. In addition, a course whose content contains a time frame, like history, may be organized in sequences corresponding to the natural progression of the events it includes. These organizational principles are logically based and have no particular concern with the goal of promoting learning, except insofar as a logically sensible organization may help to establish a favorable student attitude. In contrast to topical outlining, the defining of specific objectives, as described in the previous chapter, is most appropriately done within a topic or within a lesson. Beyond these features of logical and semantic course organization, there are three aspects of course planning that may have beneficial effects on learning. These are: (1) the use of techniques of *elaboration,* (2) the identification of *multiple learning goals,* and (3) the arrangement of *sequences of prerequisites.*

Elaboration

A particular kind of outline for a sequence of lessons making up a course is suggested by the *elaboration model of instruction* (Reigeluth & Stein, 1983). According to this view, each lesson is designed to contain such learning support features as an *epitome,* which is an overview of the simplest and most fundamental ideas of the lesson. Added to this are *elaborations,* which contribute details and show relationships within a context of related ideas. For example, in a course in economics, the epitome principle of supply and demand is introduced, and then it is illustrated by elaborations that show its relation to monopoly, price fixing, fair trade laws, and other economic events. This phase is followed by the presentation of *supportive* ideas, followed by *summary* and *synthesis* until the subject is fully explicated. The selection and sequencing of type of content, in this system, may be done by the individual learners, once they understand the functions of each type.

As for the arrangement of lessons within a course, the elaboration model proposes the following sequence:

1. Present an epitome. This is a lesson that includes a motivational strategy as a first step. Then it presents an analogy in order to represent the main idea in a familiar, concrete fashion. The lesson as a whole may then be organized approximately as indicated in the preceding paragraph.
2. Present what are called *Level 1 elaborations.* These add detail and additional organizing and supporting content to the content presented in the epit-

ome. The result, of course, is the addition of organized ideas that are conceptually subordinate to those of the epitome.

3. Present *Level 2 elaborations*. These are presented when the Level 1 lesson has been fully learned (mastered). They have the typical lesson organization, but they elaborate on some aspect of the Level 1 lesson's content, rather than on the epitome's content.

4. Present *additional levels* of elaboration. More detailed or complex levels of lessons are made available to learners as soon as previous levels have been mastered. At the end of each elaboration, an internal *summarizer* reviews the content just presented. In addition, an *expanded epitome* reviews and integrates the main content presented in earlier elaborations.

Using a class with which you are familiar, or one you expect to teach in the future, arrange a series of topics as they might be taught according to the elaboration model of instruction. Use the outline below to guide your answer.

Course Title:
Epitome:

Level 1 elaboration:

Level 2 elaboration:

Additional elaboration:

Multiple Learning Goals

The course and topic, and even the subtopic, are seldom designed to achieve a single type of learning outcome. Typically, the course or topic is expected to attain two or more of the kinds of learning goals described in Chapter 3—verbal information, intellectual skills, cognitive strategies, attitudes, and motor skills. A course in public speaking, for example, is usually designed to bring about not only the learning of rules for precise oral communication (*intellectual skills*), but also the acquisition of an *attitude* of "projecting to an audience" and probably the *cognitive strategies* involved in originating an extemporaneous speech. A course in American Government typically has multiple goals: the acquisition of *information* about the forms and procedures of government, an *attitude* of respect for democratic processes, and probably also *cognitive strategies* applicable to the solution of social problems.

It is of some importance to adequate course or topic planning, therefore, to identify various types of learning objectives and to make suitable provision for each of them. You can imagine how easy it might be to get "carried away" with the details of planning and neglect something you intended to include, even if you had begun with multiple objectives in mind. As an example, consider a teacher who wishes to design a topic with the outcomes of (1) information about harmful drugs and (2) an attitude unfavorable to the abuse of drugs. As planning proceeds, a great deal of information is collected about drugs, their composition, common names, and effects upon the human body. This information can be skillfully organized and put in a meaningful context, perhaps including tables and diagrams. When the plan is finished, it may be admired as an excellent example of a well-organized presentation. But what has become of the *attitude* as a goal? The designer will readily see that almost no provision has been made for this goal. Thus, if the topic is to fulfill both of its purposes, it must be redesigned.

Procedures of instructional planning to insure the identification and inclusion of multiple outcomes may be aided by two kinds of editing. First, one can check to see that certain important features relevant to the proposed learning outcomes have been included. (These are the critical learning conditions outlined in Chapter 5, Table 5.2). Second, by applying a question about the type of outcome, one can assure that the instruction being designed is indeed likely to reach its intended objective. Cues to both of these editing procedures are displayed in Table 6.1.

As shown in Table 6.1, the designer of a course or topic that is intended to teach *verbal information* might ask two editing questions as the design proceeds: (1) Has a meaningful context been made accessible to the learner, and are there suggested ways of encoding the information to be learned and stored? (2) When the topic has been completed, will the students be able to *state* the desired information in their own words (orally or in writing)? Similar questions pertaining to instructional features and outcomes are suggested by the table for the other types of capabilities to be learned. Their application to course and topic planning should help to maintain multiple goals for learning.

Prerequisite Sequences

Quite apart from the logical or time-ordered sequences of instructional content, the reasons for sequencing sometimes relate directly to the support of learning.

Intellectual skills typically require the prior learning of simpler

1. For the following examples of course topics, identify *at least two (2)* learning goals the teacher would be likely to have in covering the topic.

   a. In a social studies course, a topic on cultural and family differences

   b. In elementary mathematics, a topic on multiplication of one and two place numbers

   c. In a middle school gym class, a topic on the rules and strategies of playing volleyball

   d. In a high school English class, a topic on writing expository essays

2. List, for each of the goals you identified above, what performance capability you would expect of students who achieved the goals.
   a.
   b.
   c.
   d.

Answers: (1a) verbal information and attitudes; (1b) verbal information (number facts) and intellectual skills; (1c) verbal information, cognitive strategies, intellectual skills; (1d) intellectual skills and cognitive strategies. (2a) *state* information about cultural differences, and *choose* to be respectful of other cultures different from one's own; (2b) *state* the multiplication tables and *demonstrate* multiplication rules by solving problems; (2c) *state* rules of play, *identify* rules in play situations, and *originate* strategies of play that do not violate rules; (2d) *demonstrate* rules of grammar in written essays and *originate* essay topics.

TABLE 6.1   Checklist of Features for Instructional Planning of Courses and Topics for Five Types of Expected Outcomes

TYPE OF EXPECTED OUTCOME	INSTRUCTIONAL FEATURES	OUTCOME QUESTION
Verbal information	Familiar meaningful context; suggested encoding schemes, including tables and diagrams	Will the students be able to *state* the desired information?
Intellectual skill	Prior learning and retrieval of prerequisite skills: practice to mastery	Will the students be able to *demonstrate* the application of the skill?
Cognitive strategy	Presentation of strategy and occasions for using it	Will the students be able to *adopt* a task-appropriate strategy for aiding learning or thinking?
Attitude	Presentation of choice of a personal action; observation of choice and success in a human model	Will the students *choose* the intended personal action?
Motor skill	Learning of executive subroutine; practice with informative feedback	Will the students be able to *execute* the performance?

component skills (for example, see Figure 5.1). The sequences of skill learning are particularly prominent in the individual lesson, as will be described more fully in a following section. Sometimes, though, prerequisite skills may overlap several lessons or topics of a course. For example, the identification of the factors of a number may initially be learned in arithmetic as a part of the topic *multiplication,* but the skill also occurs in *division* and *fractions.* In English instruction, the agreement of verbs and pronoun subjects may initially be learned in a topic on *pronouns,* but the rule is encountered again in the topics of *sentence* and *paragraph writing.*

Other kinds of learned capabilities may also have desirable prerequisites. Sometimes, these are essential to the learning and are therefore called *enabling* prerequisites. In other instances, previously learned knowledge and skills may constitute simply *supportive* prerequisites—helpful but not essential. These relationships are shown in Table 6.2.

Some of the most readily identifiable prerequisites for the five kinds of learning outcomes are listed in Table 6.2. They are stated in general terms and intended to guide the process of course and topic planning. Not all the possible prerequisite relationships are covered by

TABLE 6.2   Prerequisite Relationships in the Design of Topics and Courses

TYPE OF OUTCOME	PREREQUISITE LEARNING
Verbal information	*Enabling:* Concept meanings, sentence syntax. *Supportive:* Related schemas of familiar information.
Intellectual skill	*Enabling:* Simpler component skills. *Supportive:* Verbal information pertaining to application.
Cognitive strategy	*Enabling:* Basic skills involved in comprehending the strategy. *Supportive:* Intellectual skills required for use of the strategy; organized knowledge.
Attitude	*Enabling:* Self-identification with human model; information and skills involved in the chosen personal action. *Supportive:* Success experience with choice of personal action.
Motor skill	*Enabling:* Executive subroutine of performance. *Supportive:* Part-skills.

the table, since variations will depend on specific circumstances. Using the table as a guide, the designer continues to address the question as to what sort of prerequisite learning had best precede any particular kind of intended learning outcome.

The learning of *verbal information,* when it is to be encoded and stored as organized knowledge, requires that the learner know (as enabling prerequisites) the meaning of the words or phrases that make up the information. That is, these words or phrases must be known as *concepts* (an intellectual skill). More than this, the learner must be able to understand sentences, which involve syntactic *rules* (for example, subject–verb–object). Suppose, for example, you were to learn and remember that "mice harbor parasites." You could encode and store this sentence provided you had previously acquired the concepts "harbor," "parasite," and "mice." You might have learned the meanings of these words during a single lesson, or they may have been introduced during an earlier topic. Besides learning these concepts, however, you would have to have the skill of understanding the sentence from its syntactic form.

Supportive types of prerequisites for verbal information are *schemas* of organized knowledge that are familiar and relevant to the new information being learned. Other features you know about mice would also support your learning that they harbor parasites. Supportive prerequisites may include images of concrete objects and events that provide cues for retrieval of the newly learned knowledge. In their totality, they provide the meaningful context for the learning (Table 6.1).

As already indicated, the learning of an *intellectual skill* requires prior learning of simpler component skills. The application of the skill to particular examples may be supported by previously learned verbal information specific to the examples. For instance, the intellectual skill of *solving a proportion* might be applied in a problem such as the following: "What force is required to bring a lever into equilibrium about a fulcrum when the force on one end is twenty grams, three meters from the fulcrum, and the force to be found is applied at the other end, five meters from the fulcrum?" Obviously, applying the appropriate rule for proportion in this instance will demand that the learner have prior information relating concepts such as *lever, fulcrum,* and *equilibrium* to each other. Such information is likely to have been introduced by plan in a previous topic.

Enabling skills for the learning of *cognitive strategies* are simply those needed by the learner in comprehending the procedure of the strategy itself. Strategies that are communicated verbally, as in "Remember the first letter of each word," or "Think of an image that connects these events," or "Break the problem down into parts" obviously require that the learner comprehend these communications, and that implies some basic language skills. The adoption and use of a cognitive strategy may also demand access to previously acquired intellectual skills and verbal information. Summarizing text may be adopted by a learner who possesses the skill of summarizing; generating a memorable image is a strategy that may require prior practice in imaging.

Still another function of previously learned information can be identified as supportive of the adoption of cognitive strategies, particularly in the case of strategies of thinking (or problem solving). Research studies have often shown that originality of thought is related to amount of organized knowledge that people possess (Johnson, 1972). Most truly original thinkers are people who have vast stores of knowledge in many fields. Thus, the accessibility of verbal information, whether learned in previous topics of a course or in other courses, is likely to be supportive of the development of productive thinking strategies.

Attitude learning or modification requires as a prerequisite that the learner respect or otherwise "identify" with a human model. As pointed out in Chapter 5, this model is usually an admired person, fictional or real. In early grades of school, the teacher is usually the most important model, who communicates the desirable choice of personal action. A positive attitude toward *helping others,* for example, may be initially introduced in a small way, by encouraging a child to find a chair for a classmate. This incident (presumably pleasant) may then be used at a later time for more elaborate behavior choices of helping.

Information and skills involved in the chosen personal action are also enabling prerequisites to the development of attitudes. This is because the behavior aimed for must be within the student's repertoire as established by prior learning. Finally, supportive aspects of previously acquired behavior depend upon the experience of success following the choice of personal action. A learner is more likely to acquire a positive attitude toward an action that was rewarded for being successful in the past.

In learning a *motor skill,* the executive subroutine that controls the sequence of responses may have been previously learned, or else it must be learned initially. In learning to turn an automobile around on a two-lane road, for example, the executive procedure of forward turning left—backward turning right—forward turning left, and so on must be kept constantly in mind by the novice driver, as practice continues in the motor skill of controlling the car's movement by means of the accelerator pedal and steering wheel. Still another kind of learning which may be planned for an earlier stage of a course is the learning of part-skills. In swimming instruction, for example, the part-skill involving leg movement is often practiced separately from the total skill of the crawl, before being put together with other part-skills.

Thus, the planning of sequences of instructional components that compose a course or topic frequently requires attention to *prerequisites.* The course planner is concerned with the question of whether each new lesson or topic has been preceded by the learning of capabilities that adequately prepare the learner to undertake the new learning. Since new learning is often a matter of combining capabilities that can be made accessible in memory, course planning must insure that these capabilities have been previously learned.

PLANNING THE LESSON

Once topics and subtopics have been identified and placed in a suitable sequence, instructional planning can proceed to concern itself with the individual unit of instruction, which we call the lesson. As conceived here, the lesson has no fixed time characteristics, nor can the scope of its coverage be specified exactly. In the typical classroom setting, the lesson is often planned to require the time of a class period, say forty-five or fifty minutes. However, a lesson may also be designed as a student project, which is expected to be accomplished in several hours spread over a longer period of time—days or weeks. Or, a lesson may be a single laboratory exercise to be undertaken by a pair of students or a small group and to extend over several class periods. As noted previously, a single lesson may be concerned with more than one type of learning outcome. In general, when an intellectual skill like "writing a unified

For each of the following examples of learning goals, list at least one prerequisite students must have in order to successfully achieve the goal.

1. *Goal:* Solve problems such as, "How much time would it take to travel 75 miles if one were moving at a speed of 50 mph?"
   prerequisite:

2. *Goal:* Classify types of animals (e.g., mammal, reptile, insect, bird)
   prerequisite:

3. *Goal:* Execute the crawl stroke (swimming)
   prerequisite:

Possible Answers:

(1) Concepts such as time, speed, distance must have been learned, as well as arithmetic rules and expressing fractional numbers.

(2) The concepts of mammal, reptile, insect, bird must have been learned, along with the concepts that represent distinguishing attributes of these concepts (e.g., "bears live young," "lay eggs," "flies," etc.)

(3) The part-skills of this motor skill must have been acquired before it can be performed in its entirety. Thus, the arm stroke, leg kick, or breathing rhythm are all possible answers.

paragraph" is the primary goal, the same lesson may also give some attention to an attitude such as "preferring to read self-produced paragraphs that have unity." In addition, such a lesson may well be concerned with the adoption of one or more cognitive strategies when it includes an assignment such as "Write an original paragraph describing the effects of a sudden, unexpected event such as a loud clap of thunder." Practical instruction seldom attains the purity of a single type of learning outcome.

The Events of a Lesson

Planning a lesson is mainly a matter of taking care to assure that each of the internal learning processes (Chapter 2) has been supported in an optimal fashion by *external events*. One must keep in mind the expected type of learning outcome and the special conditions each requires (Table 6.1). In a more particular sense, attention must be paid to the series of external events that can influence learning processes, as described in Chapter 2. The events to be described in the following paragraphs follow that outline of learning processes. The events of the lesson occur roughly in an order as follows, although this order is not considered an inviolable one:

1. Gaining attention
2. Informing the learner of the objective
3. Stimulating recall of prior learning
4. Presenting the stimulus
5. Providing learning guidance
6. Eliciting performance
7. Providing feedback
8. Assessing performance
9. Enhancing retention and transfer.

The following paragraphs describe in general terms the activities that may be employed to bring these events into play.

1. Gaining attention.   This external event has the purpose of alerting the student to the reception of stimuli. In general, attention is gained by the introduction of rapid stimulus change—a change in room brightness, a sudden sound, an alteration in the pitch of a teacher's voice, or any of a variety of changes of this general nature. Teachers customarily use common methods of gaining attention for a room full of children (clapping hands, giving verbal signals) or for smaller groups and individuals (calling the student by name). Sometimes, the alerting stimulus may be related to the content of the lesson, as when a flashing red light is used to introduce a lesson on street-crossing procedures, or when the recorded sound of a crow opens a lesson on bird calls. This type of attention-getting can serve well, also, to make an easy transition to the next event of a lesson.

2. Informing the learner of the objective.   Learners need to know the aim of learning, in the sense of what they will be able to do once learning has been accomplished. This knowledge establishes an *expectancy* that the learner will be able to acquire the new capability, and thus contributes to self-efficacy, as the ARCS model provides (Chapter 4). In addition, the expectancy anticipates successful attainment of the performance being learned, and thus continues to be an incentive for learner effort.

Relating the expected learning outcome to student interests is also a part of the purpose of informing students about the objective. Sometimes, it may be possible to relate with a general motivational state, as when students are led to see that knowing how to identify microorganisms with a microscope (the objective) will enable them to detect water impurities. But beyond this, a specific expectancy of the learning outcome of the lesson usually needs to be established. This may be done when the teacher, or the textbook, communicates to the learners *what they will be able to do* when learning has been completed. Referring again to the

FIGURE 6.1. Informing learners of the objective.

microscope lesson, students may be told that when learning is completed, they will be able to identify several specified types of microorganisms in pond water. If the lesson is in arithmetic, the communication to students may establish the expectancy that they will (when learning is complete) be able to divide a fraction by a fraction; if in language, students may come to realize that they will be able to demonstrate the use of *who* and *whom*.

3. Stimulating recall of prior learning. Before the new learning takes place, an additional kind of event needs to be instituted as a part of instruction. This stimulates *retrieval* of previously learned items. As we emphasized earlier in this chapter, various previously learned capabilities (prerequisites) need to be made readily accessible in the learner's working memory. Different means may be employed to stimulate retrieval of these previously learned entities. One can simply say, "Remember that you learned how to interpolate values between those shown on

FIGURE 6.2. Stimulating recall of prior learning.

a scale"; or "Remember what *freezing* means." Communications of this type often accomplish the purpose of making prerequisite learnings accessible from the student's memory.

Sometimes, however, the recall of necessary capabilities may require more than a simple reminder—for instance, when the prior learning has occurred a fairly long time ago or when there has been inadequate opportunity for intervening review. In such instances, a more elaborate event, in which students actively *reinstate* what has previously been learned, may need to be arranged. Thus, before proceeding with a lesson whose objective is "making personal pronouns agree with verbs," the teacher may first set the task: "Write a list of all the personal pronouns." This list would then be checked over by the students, with feedback from the teacher, to insure that all had fully recalled the pronouns and thus were ready to proceed with the new learning. Or, if the lesson had the objective of "classifying types of urban transportation," the teacher might find it desirable to have the students recall the definition of a city. The students might be asked to "Write an outline to show how the definition of a city applies to _____ [a city shown in an aerial photograph]." Again, this exercise would have the purpose of assuring the retrieval of previously learned capabilities.

4. Presenting the stimulus. The stimulus presented as a lesson event depends on what is to be learned. If verbal information is to be acquired, the stimulus may be a printed text or an audio message containing the content. If an intellectual skill is to be learned, an object or a set of symbols representing the concept or rule may be displayed. A cognitive strategy can be communicated verbally, demonstrated, or both. For a motor skill, the essential movements and their objective may be demonstrated. In the case of an attitude, the stimulus consists of the human model and the message the model delivers.

In any of these instances, the most effective stimulus is one in which *distinctive features* are made prominent. In many instances, this may be done by simple communications such as "Look at the even numbers in this series," or "Notice the subject and the verb in this sentence."

More precise methods of emphasizing distinctive features may also be employed, with the aim of aiding selective perception. When the sounds of letters are being learned by children, for example, greater intensity may be given to sounding of specific letters within syllables, as in "A, rA, rAt"—when the sound of the vowel "a" is to be learned. If the growing parts of a plant are to be identified as an objective of a science lesson, these parts may be separately outlined and labeled in a diagram to which the student refers while making his observations. In the learning of a geometric rule such as "Triangles are similar when two of the angles

FIGURE 6.3.   Presenting the stimulus, emphasizing distinctive features.

of each are equal," the angles of two triangles may be outlined heavily in a diagram so that attention is drawn to them.

5. Providing learning guidance.   This is the lesson event that should bring about *semantic encoding* and the entry of what is to be learned into long-term memory. Generally speaking, the set of events that form a part of instruction during this phase of learning is called *learning guidance*. These events are differentiated in their substance, in accordance with the particular kind of learning outcome intended, as indicated in Table 5.2. Thus, if the learning of verbal information is the intended outcome, the accompanying learning guidance takes the form of a meaningful context; if a rule is to be learned, guidance may be provided by a verbal statement cueing the sequence in which subordinate rules are to be combined; and so on. In general, guidance may take the form of suggestions for organizing the content, associating it with other materials by elaboration, or indicating mnemonic techniques.

The amount of learning guidance provided, that is, the length and complexity of the communication or other form of stimulation, varies

FIGURE 6.4. Providing learning guidance.

with a number of factors in the situation. For example, to a group of bright students applying newly learned arithmetic rules to verbally stated examples, the teacher may find it desirable to provide a minimal amount of guidance, or none at all, and thus to emphasize *discovery learning.* For somewhat less able students, guidance might take the form of *hints* or *prompts,* which carefully avoid "giving the answer away." Turning to a different kind of learning, motor skills, it is evident that learning guidance may concern itself with the cueing of the executive subroutine, as in "taking the proper stance." Beyond this, however, verbal guidance is known to be of little use for motor skills; the learner must practice the motor act itself.

Perhaps the most general common characteristic to be sought in learning guidance is its orientation to the objective. In whatever form it is given, whether as verbal statements, hints, diagrams, or pictures, its purpose is to assure a form of *encoding* that will enable the learner later to recover what has been learned and display it as some kind of performance. It is essential that examples of situations are included which will later be encountered by the student and which become sources of cues to retrieval. Thus, the verbal communication, set of cues, or diagram chosen to provide learning guidance is not to be selected because of its logical or esthetic qualities, but rather because it *helps the learner to store and recall* what is being learned.

6. Eliciting performance.   The events of a lesson described to this point are designed to assure that learning does indeed occur. The new capability of the objective, whether verbal information, intellectual skill, cognitive strategy, attitude, or motor skill, has presumably been encoded for storage in the learner's long-term memory. This is the time for learners to confirm, for themselves, the teacher, and others, that the intended learning has taken place. The external event, then, is one of asking the learner to exhibit what has been learned. Asking a verbally stated question, of course, may be the most straightforward way of eliciting the performance. But there are many other ways that may be used to place the learner into a situation that requires a performance.

7. Providing feedback.   Having learned, students need to "show what they can do," not only for the teacher's purposes, but also for their own learning. The display of the performance should be closely coupled

FIGURE 6.5.   Eliciting performance.

with *informative feedback,* in order for reinforcement to occur. This phrase implies informing the learner of the degree of correctness or incorrectness of the performance. For example, if the student has learned the skill of locating a position on a globe in terms of latitude and longitude, the problem might be set as one of finding the position of the city of St. Louis. When latitude and longitude of the city are reported, the student is then given feedback as to whether these are correct, or to what extent and in what way they differ from the correct values.

8. Assessing performance. A single correct performance reflecting the new learning is barely adequate. In order to have greater confidence that the establishment of a new capability is *dependable,* the teacher usually asks the student to demonstrate the performance a number of times. When a rule has been newly learned, for instance, the student may be asked to apply it to several different examples, one after another. If an attitude toward "finishing the task" has been learned, the student may be asked to indicate choice of this personal action in connection with a variety of different tasks. These additional instances of eliciting the performance may be viewed as a test of the adequacy (and reliability) of learning. Viewed simply as a late event in a lesson, however, it would be desirable that each correct performance be given suitable feedback.

9. Enhancing retention and transfer. Instructional provisions for enhancing retention and retrieval of what has been learned take the form of *spaced reviews.* Spacing means requiring recall at reasonable intervals, of a day or more, following the initial learning. It is customary, for instance, to provide a number of examples calling for application of a newly learned capability immediately after learning is completed. Requiring more than two or three review examples is relatively ineffective, however, so long as the examples are to be done immediately. The recall of the learned capability is greatly enhanced, however, when additional examples are spaced in time over days or weeks following the initial learning.

It is desirable for spaced reviews to include a variety of situations. For example, if the student has initially learned to form ratios in connection with areas, the examples employed in spaced reviews might be designed to require application to ratios of distance/time, and voltage/resistance, and weight/volume. If the student has learned to define "legislative" in terms of the national Congress, examples in spaced reviews might require application of the definition to state legislatures and city councils. Variety in examples is known to enhance retention, presumably because it enables students to acquire additional internal cues that they can use to search their memories.

FIGURE 6.6.   Eliciting performance; providing feedback.

In making use of learning transfer to promote new learning within a course or subject (transfer in the *vertical* sense), it is essential to provide for the prior learning of prerequisite information and intellectual skills. For this reason, a lesson may include questions or problems that have the double purpose of: (1) probing for the presence of these prerequisite capabilities, and (2) making sure they are currently available in the student's "working memory." Such activities may not always occupy much time, but they are of critical importance in making use of the advantage learning transfer gives to the acquisition of new capabilities.

When transfer of learning to other fields of study or activity (*lateral* transfer) is aimed for, support is provided by a variety of examples and situations. In large part, transfer of the lateral sort appears to depend upon the effectiveness of memory search and retrieval carried out by the learner when he confronts new situations to which his previously learned capabilities must be applied. Accordingly, the promotion of transfer is brought about by instruction that provides novel tasks for the student, spaced over time, and calling for the use of what has previously been learned. Often, these novel tasks take the form of problem-solving situations—undertaking a project, composing an essay, solving a mathematical puzzle, designing an investigation of a natural phenomenon.

FIGURE 6.7.   Enhancing retention and transfer.

Relating Instructional Events to Learning Processes

Each external event of instruction is designed to support one or more of the internal processes of learning. This point has been the subject of Chapter 5 and has been reemphasized in the description of each lesson event contained in preceding paragraphs. A pictorial representation of these relationships is given in Figure 6.8. In this figure, the processes of learning (derived from the model of Figure 2.1) are shown opposite the events of instruction that support the processes. The figure provides a summary of instructional events, and indicates their timing in relation to the processes they are designed to influence.

SELF-INSTRUCTION AND LEARNING

As we have emphasized throughout this book, the instructional events designed to be carried out during an act of learning (several of which may occur during a single lesson) have the purpose of stimulating, activating, supporting, and facilitating the internal processes of learning. Any of these events may be useful in achieving these purposes for any specific lesson or lesson component, or all of them may be. However, it

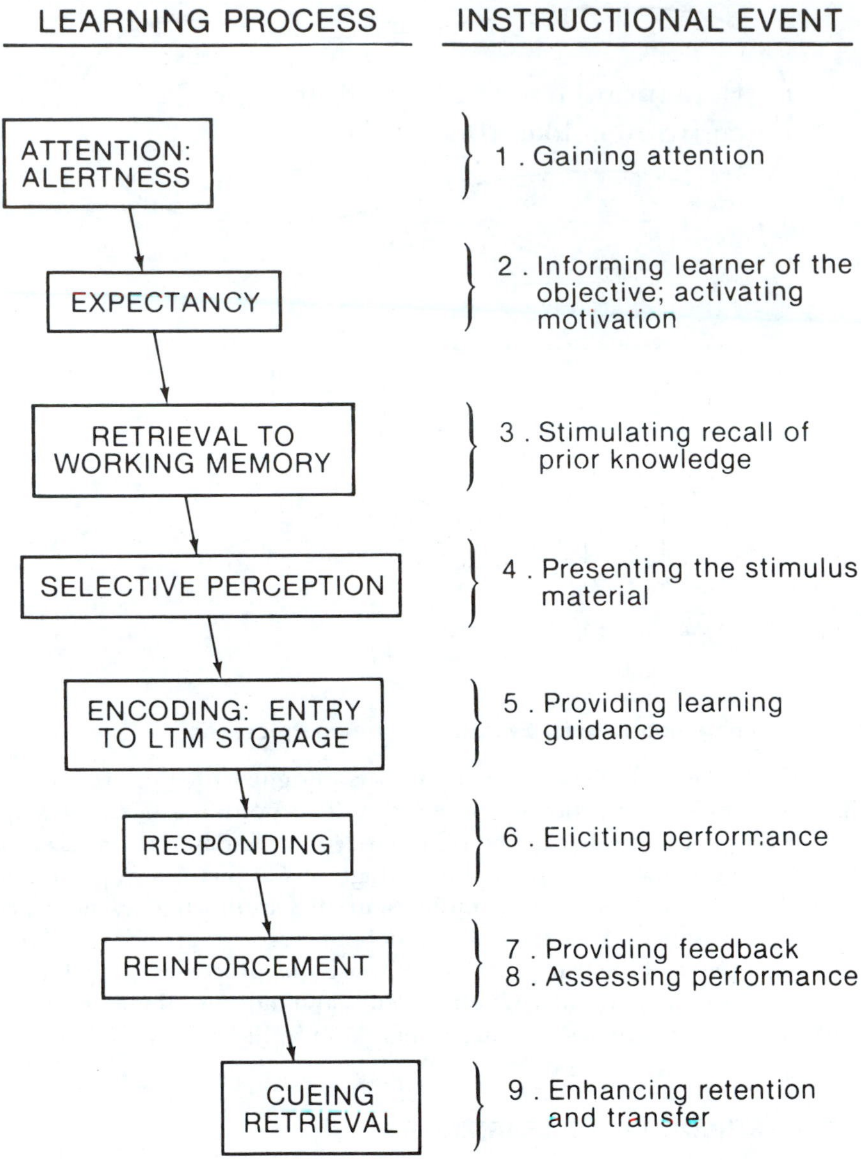

LEARNING PROCESS   INSTRUCTIONAL EVENT

LEARNING PROCESS	INSTRUCTIONAL EVENT
ATTENTION: ALERTNESS	1 . Gaining attention
EXPECTANCY	2 . Informing learner of the objective; activating motivation
RETRIEVAL TO WORKING MEMORY	3 . Stimulating recall of prior knowledge
SELECTIVE PERCEPTION	4 . Presenting the stimulus material
ENCODING: ENTRY TO LTM STORAGE	5 . Providing learning guidance
RESPONDING	6 . Eliciting performance
REINFORCEMENT	7 . Providing feedback 8 . Assessing performance
CUEING RETRIEVAL	9 . Enhancing retention and transfer

FIGURE 6.8.   Relations between phases of learning and events of instruction. The latter events represent the functions performed by instruction which support internal learning processes. (From Gagné, R. M. [1985]. *The conditions of learning,* 4th ed. Reprinted by permission of the copyright owner, Holt, Rinehart & Winston, Inc.)

Classify each of the following examples as to which of the nine events of instruction it illustrates.

1. Gaining attention
2. Informing the learner of the objective
3. Stimulating recall of prior knowledge
4. Presenting the stimulus material
5. Providing learning guidance
6. Eliciting performance
7. Providing feedback
8. Assessing performance
9. Enhancing retention and transfer

————a. A physical education teacher corrects errors as students practice their tennis serves.

————b. A computer lesson begins with, "Can you plan your weekly budget, knowing your salary and expenses? When you finish this lesson, you will be able to!"

————c. A social studies teacher taps a large wall map to begin a lesson on world geography.

————d. At the end of each week, a foreign language instructor gives students new sentences to translate that contain the vocabulary words learned in the previous week.

————e. A textbook chapter contains diagrams of trees with arrows pointing to labeled features such as bark, branches, roots, and leaves.

————f. A primary school teacher brings in many objects that are very familiar to the children when he is teaching the concept of "round."

Answers: (a) 7; (b) 2; (c) 1; (d) 9; (e) 4; (f) 5

should be clear that the particular events that need to be planned for any given learner, or for any group of learners, cannot be predicted with precision. Individual differences among students are large, at all ages, and must be taken fully into account in the planning of instruction.

Differences in Self-Instruction

The student differences of particular relevance to the planning of instruction are those pertaining to the *amount of self-instruction* the students are able to undertake. Obviously, skilled adults, such as college seniors or university graduate students, arrange virtually all the events of instruction for themselves. For them, learning is typically a matter of reading a book or several books. If they are truly sophisticated learners, they are already motivated. They set their own objectives, perceive the distinctive features of the stimulus, use efficient encoding procedures, devise novel ways of applying what they have learned, demonstrate to themselves the performances of which they are capable, and verify the effects of these performances as a source of feedback. These are the *learning strategies* that have been acquired through years of experiences with successful learning, and which may have been taught in a direct fashion initially (Chapter 7).

Many learners, however, are not as skilled as the true "self-learner." Instead, they may still be acquiring the metacognitive procedures of learning (summarization, concentration management, and other "study habits") that activate and guide their own learning processes. The external events of instruction are designed (1) to provide the support needed in activating learning processes, and (2) to encourage the development of the cognitive strategies that will make such external support largely unnecessary. This latter is not an easy goal to attain, and it cannot be done over short periods of time (see Chapter 7). According to experience as currently appraised, developing a student into a truly independent learner takes years. This is a basic reason why organized programs of instruction exists—to fill these years with learning.

Choosing Instructional Events

The instructional events the teacher chooses to omit from the total set listed in Figure 6.8 should be those that, as an estimate, are not required because the students can supply them themselves. First graders, in general, would not be expected to be capable of managing their own learning processes. Sixth graders may be able to assume sets to direct attention and to use moderately effective strategies of coding and retrieval. High school students should be able to instruct themselves in many of the capabilities they are expected to learn. But these are generalities only. The teacher must decide, for each specific learning act, which instructional events might be omitted and which need to be emphasized.

The following list is intended as a guide for estimates of the potentiality for self-instruction and, therefore, for the planning of instructional events:

1. *Gaining attention* can be omitted as an event when the motivation of learners can be assumed. For much of instruction, though, it is an essential event.

2. *Informing learners of the objective* of a lesson is almost always a good idea, except when the objective is already apparent.

3. *Stimulating recall of prior learning* is usually a critical event, although it may not be necessary for skillful self-learners.

4. *Presenting the stimulus* is of course always essential and is usually made more effective when features are made highly distinctive.

5. *Providing learning guidance.* This is the event that most typically may be provided by the learner's use of cognitive strategies in self-instruction.

6. *Eliciting performance.* Skillful learners virtually always assure themselves of their own performance capabilities.

7. *Providing feedback* is a step that usually accompanies the performance. Learners who are engaging in self-instruction will seek accurate information about the adequacy of their performances. It is this event that completes the learning, and to omit it would be a serious mistake.

8. *Assessing performance* will usually be done by experienced learners in following up the initial performance event.

9. *Enhancing retention and transfer* requires additional practice with a variety of examples and situations. These will need to be supplied for most learners, but may often be independently sought out by learners who are organizing their own instruction.

Obviously, including more instructional events than are necessary is likely to lead to boredom on the part of students. Providing fewer than are needed, however, has the serious consequences of inadequate learning, misdirected learning, or no learning at all. Making good estimates of student self-instructional capabilities is an essential part of instructional planning.

Summary Exercise

Generate an instructional objective that you might someday teach in your field. Identify which type of learning outcome your objective represents. Then describe how you might implement each of the nine events of instruction in order to effectively teach the objective. Be sure to give a rationale for any event you choose not to include in your instruction.

GENERAL REFERENCES

Learning and Instruction

Gagné, E. D. (1985). *The cognitive psychology of school learning.* Boston: Little, Brown.
Gagné, R. M. (1985). *The conditions of learning,* 4th ed. New York: Holt, Rinehart and Winston.

Instructional Planning

Briggs, L. J. (Ed.). (1977). *Instructional design: Principles and applications.* Englewood Cliffs, NJ: Educational Technology.

Briggs, L. J., & Wager, W. W. (1981). *Handbook of procedures for the design of instruction.* Englewood Cliffs, NJ: Educational Technology.

Gagné, R. M., Briggs, L. J., & Wager, W. W. (1988). *Principles of instructional design,* 3rd ed. New York: Holt, Rinehart and Winston.

Popham, W. J., & Baker, E. L. (1970). *Planning an instructional sequence.* Englewood Cliffs, NJ: Prentice Hall.

Tyler, R. W. (1949). *Basic principles of curriculum and instruction.* Chicago: University of Chicago Press.

SEVEN
LEARNER STRATEGIES

A high priority goal often cited for education is to teach students to be self-learners and independent thinkers. In Chapter 2, we introduced the idea that learners can become independent thinkers by using self-generated strategies that will activate or support the internal processes of learning. Broadly conceived, *cognitive strategies* are the set of capabilities we have described in Chapter 3 that make possible this *executive control* of learning processes. When a learner employs cognitive strategies during a learning task, the outcome may be considered to be an original or creative product or solution. (See Chapter 3 for an account of cognitive strategies as learning outcomes.)

When the focus shifts from the performance outcome that is evidence of cognitive strategies to the question of how learners can supply these strategies for themselves, the latter subset is made up of *learner strategies*. Learner strategies are those procedures learners employ to provide the events of instruction for themselves. In using them, regardless of whether the learning goal is chosen by the learner or selected by the teacher, the learner is engaging in *self-instruction*.

In this chapter, we will present examples of learner strategies that have been shown to be effective in self-learning situations. The examples illustrate how learners may supply the events of instruction for themselves, as well as how they can influence their own motivational and emotional states. We shall also consider how these strategies may be acquired by or taught to learners.

STRATEGIES FOR INTERNAL PROCESSING

A student who has decided to learn a particular objective, whether it is stated in a textbook or selected by the student, may start with a general plan as to how to proceed. This general plan essentially embodies the events of instruction and consists of those particular strategies related to each event that are known by the learner. But the plan will also be influenced by the learner's own awareness of thinking processes and how to appropriately employ these processes in order to achieve a learning goal. This awareness of thinking is called *metacognition* (Brown, 1980) and it plays a critical role in the learner's ability to develop self-instruction skills (Pressley, Borkowski, & O'Sullivan, 1984).

To give you a better idea as to what metacognition entails, consider this example. Suppose individual students wanted to learn more about the events that served as catalysts to the Industrial Revolution (learning outcome). They could probably do this by reading in a book, listening to an audio tape, viewing a filmstrip, or by some other means (instructional condition). If they found it easy to learn from visual types of instruction and were aware that generating a diagram of related events would help in learning (metacognition), they might choose to view the film and then draw a sketch depicting related events (learner strategy). Thus, the choice of a particular strategy within the general plan may depend on the individual learner's metacognition.

Attentional Strategies

The first event of instruction is to gain and direct the attention of the learner. The self-instructing student may adopt one of several attentional strategies, depending upon the objective to be learned. *Underlining* key points (Rickards & August, 1975) is one way the student may focus attention on information to be learned. This strategy presupposes, of course, that the student is reading a printed text. It is a strategy that works best with older learners. Brown and Smiley (1977), for example, found that children below the sixth grade could not adequately identify the important information and therefore did not benefit from an underlining strategy.

Students may also adopt an attentional set, which means that they read, listen, or look selectively for the communications they need. Think,

for an example, of students who wish to learn about the mating and nesting behavior of ospreys. In searching for relevant books, films, public
television nature shows, and the like, they would selectively look for "os-
prey," followed by "mating and nesting."

In any event, self-instructing students employ attentional strategies
after they have determined what objective is to be learned (the second
event of instruction). As stated earlier, they may be learning on their own
some objective selected by the teacher, or they may have decided upon
their own objective. You are no doubt familiar with many examples of
self-study projects or homework assignments that have been selected and
assigned by a teacher. Learners choosing their own objectives is a common feature of secondary and adult education programs, in which
learners may seek out specialized learning experiences.

Strategies to Enhance Short-Term Storage

In order to offset the limitations of storage and time capacities of
short-term memory, students may adopt rehearsal or chunking strategies.
Rehearsal strategies, such as repeating a list or copying text, serve to keep
information available for further processing to long-term memory and
are most often used for memorizing. Studies indicate that even young
children can benefit from using a rehearsal strategy on memory tasks,
but may have to be reminded to use the strategy (Flavell, 1970; Flavell &
Wellman, 1977).

Older students may use repetitive rehearsal as a study strategy to
the exclusion of strategies more appropriate for the learning goal. Suppose, for example, you had to summarize and interpret research studies
such as those reported in this book. Rehearsal of the text might aid you
with the first part of this goal—that is, summarizing— but the strategy
would not help you to accomplish the second part of the goal, interpreting. Interpreting requires that you draw inferences, and to do this, you
must have encoded and integrated the information stored as prior knowledge. A strategy such as rehearsal, which is designed to support only
short-term storage, would therefore not be appropriate.

Another set of strategies used to enhance short-term storage are
called *chunking strategies*. Chunking strategies enable students to hold
more information in short-term memory, so that more can be processed
for long-term storage. For example, faced with a list of animals to be
learned, a student may organize them by taxonomic category—mammals,
birds, reptiles, and insects.

For more complex learning goals, students may employ such techniques as diagramming or outlining in order to chunk concepts and information. Topic outlining, for example, helps students to build internal
connections among major and minor points, particularly in expository

prose. Using key words or phrases, students first identify the main ideas in a text passage. Then they identify the minor ideas or details that support each of the main ideas. The completed topic outline thus provides the student with the informational chunks to be learned from the text.

Strategies to Enhance Encoding

Learner strategies to enhance encoding are embodied in the events of instruction: stimulating recall of prior learning, presenting the stimulus, and providing learning guidance. The first two of these events are instituted when the learners remind themselves of the meanings of prerequisite concepts and find the material appropriate for the learning goal. Recall the example of students learning about catalysts to the Industrial Revolution. They might remind themselves of the meaning of "catalyst." They would then select the medium by which the desired information could be gained (in our example, film). And finally, they would employ one or more learner strategies to help encode the meaning of the new information (in our example, drawing a diagram).

Just as you, as a teacher, would select instructional strategies appropriate to a given learning outcome, so you, as a learner, would select learner strategies to aid the learning of a given outcome. Suppose, for example, you wanted to learn the association, "On a boat, port means left and starboard means right." You might use a mnemonic such as: "Port and left have the same number of letters; right and starboard have more." Mnemonic strategies can be quite useful in learning simple facts (see, for example, reviews by Higbee, 1979, and Bellezza, 1981).

For more complex learning goals, the self-instructing learner might employ such tactics as creating analogies to things already known, drawing implications, creating verbal or imaginal relationships, questioning, and paraphrasing (Weinstein, 1982). For example, a student trying to understand how information is stored by a computer might say to himself, "This is like the operation of a post office; information is sent to the *address* it is given."

A particularly effective encoding technique used by self-instructing students is the strategy of thinking up questions to ask oneself (or others). Students reading a textbook chapter describing events that preceded the dropping of the first atomic bomb, for example, might ask themselves such questions as, "Who decided the bomb should be dropped?" "What political and economic conditions existed in the world at this time?" "What were the most critical factors that may have influenced the decision?" "Are there parallel conditions existing in the world today?", and so on. Some of these questions aid students in comprehending the meaning of the text passage. Others, which call for drawing inferences, help students to integrate the new information with what they have previously learned.

Asking themselves inferential questions, students may also engage in problem-solving. For example, asking "What can individuals do today to avoid nuclear war?" may lead to the generation of possible solutions and courses of action. The result, in any event, is improved encoding because an effective elaboration strategy has been employed in learning.

Strategies to Enhance Retrieval

To assist retrieval, students may use many of the same strategies they employed to help encoding. For example, suppose a learner decided that creating an image was a good way to learn how nutrients in a plant are transported through the stem to the leaves. This same image would serve the learner well when it came to remembering this information at a later time. Similarly, analogies, mnemonics, or questions that a learner has generated can serve to aid retrieval of what was encoded.

A common strategy for enhancing retrieval with which most students are very familiar is notetaking. This is sometimes called an external retrieval strategy (Kiewra, 1985) because the product of notetaking—notes—serves as storage external to the individual. Different systems for taking notes exist, and it appears that students who use one of these systems typically perform better than students left to their own devices (Carrier & Titus, 1981). Students who relate their notes in some way to material covered previously also tend to perform better than students who do not elaborate on their notes (Peper & Mayer, 1978).

Note: In the exercises for this chapter, you will sometimes be asked to take the perspective of a *learner,* and at other times the perspective of a *teacher.*

1. Suppose you wanted to learn about the land animals that inhabit the area in which you live. What specific strategies might you employ to enhance your *attention, encoding, and retrieval* processes for learning this goal? Compare your answers with those of another student, and justify your differences.

2. Name one or more learning goals for which using strategies to facilitate *short-term storage* would be particularly important. Indicate whether the goals would be aided by *rehearsal* or *chunking* strategies, and explain why.

Monitoring Strategies

Self-instructing students "know" when they have achieved the objective they have set out to learn. This is another aspect of metacognition, described earlier. During the process of learning, students employ monitoring strategies to check their understanding of what they have read, heard, or seen. Can you recall an experience in which you "read" an entire paragraph or page and then suddenly realized you had not comprehended a single word? While the monitoring of your comprehension probably seemed automatic and unconscious in that experience, self-instructing students also monitor their understanding in a quite conscious fashion. They may check themselves with questions such as "Did I understand that?" or "What did that mean?"

Once the learning process is complete, learners may check themselves with self-tests, such as questions to answer or new problems to solve. In doing this, learners are able to confirm the expectancy with which they began the learning task and thus supply for themselves the events of instruction: elicit performance and provide feedback. A learner skilled in strategies for learning transfer may also establish some broader generalizations of what was learned and seek problems that would confirm that transfer had occurred. In this way, the learner might discover, and keep track of, relationships not contained in the original material viewed or read.

Summary: The General Plan

At the beginning of this section, we indicated that learners typically approach a learning task with a general plan. The contents of the plan will depend upon the particular strategies known by the learner and what the learner knows about using them appropriately (metacognition). We have thus far described a variety of learner strategies, their functions, and appropriate applications. To implement a plan, however, learners will also use their knowledge of the learning task requirements and the learning environment. Let us take a look at how this overall plan may operate.

Five steps comprise the overall approach taken by self-instructing students when tackling a learning goal (Derry & Murphy, 1986). They are:

1. *Identify and analyze the goal.* In this first step, learners determine salient aspects of the learning task (*what* is to be learned) and assess the demands of the learning environment (*when* and *where* is it to be accomplished and according to what standards).
2. *Plan the strategy.* On the basis of the analysis conducted in Step 1, the self-instructing learner now formulates a *plan,* consisting of a strategy or set of strategies with which to accomplish the desired learning. In other words,

the learner thinks, "Given this type of task, to be accomplished in this way, I should use these learning tactics."

3. *Carry out the strategy.* At this step, the learner employs the strategy or strategies determined to help in accomplishing the learning goal.

4. *Monitor the results of the strategy.* Once the learning process is underway, self-instructing learners monitor the degree to which the strategies they have chosen are having the intended effect. For example, they may ask themselves, "Is this image, or this mnemonic technique, successful in helping me remember what I need to know?"

5. *Modify the strategy.* If the answer to the questions posed in Step 4 is "Yes, the strategy is working to assist learning," then the learner may decide no change is necessary. However, if the strategy does not appear to be producing satisfactory results, the learner must reevaluate and modify the original analysis of the goal or the plan.

STRATEGIES FOR MOTIVATION

In the previous section, we focused on what learners do to affect their own cognitive processes in order to accomplish some learning task or goal. Sometimes, however, learners may supply appropriate events of instruction for themselves and yet still experience difficulty achieving their goals. These difficulties could stem from motivational or emotional, rather than cognitive, factors. They call for *affective* strategies.

The model of motivation presented in Chapter 4 can serve as a framework for discussing some affective strategies self-instructing students may employ to overcome motivational or emotional barriers to learning. The ARCS model proposes that four conditions must be met within the learner in order for motivation to be optimal for learning: *A*ttention, *R*elevance, *C*onfidence, and *S*atisfaction.

Affective Strategies for Maintaining Attention

One of the most common problems students face in self-learning situations is simple distraction from their task. Distractions often come in the form of external interruptions, as when your roommate comes in and turns on the stereo while you are reading or studying. To counter this type of distraction, some investigators (Dansereau, 1985) have suggested methods of *mood management*. For one thing, students can set the right mood for learning by determining and arranging the environmental characteristics that best support their learning. This could mean finding a quiet spot in the library, arranging one's desk in a particular way, always studying at the dining room table, or listening to background music through earphones. Any strategy that helps a learner avoid or minimize unwanted disruptions can serve to enhance the motivational condition of maintaining attention.

Distractions can also come from within the learner, as when you think to yourself, "I cannot understand this. I will probably do poorly on this project." This negative self-talk can lead to decreased motivation and thus decreased attention to the task at hand. Strategies to counter negative self-statements constitute a second aspect of mood management. Meichenbaum (1977) suggests that students learn to recognize these counterproductive statements and substitute more positive ones. In fact, practicing positive self-talk can gradually lead an individual away from a self-defeating attitude toward more highly motivated behavior.

Affective Strategies to Enhance Relevance

Skilled self-instructing learners are generally quite adept at identifying what is relevant to them about a given learning task. They may ask themselves questions such as, "Why is this, or should this be, important to me?" or "What value does this hold for me, either now or in the future?" Answering these questions in a positive way helps learners to maintain interest and enthusiasm for what they are learning.

Another strategy self-instructing learners employ to enhance the relevance of learning is to continually seek ways of integrating the newly learned material with what they have already learned or are learning in other contexts. In other words, they ask themselves, "How does this fit with what I already know?" If discrepancies seem to exist between new and previously learned ideas, the self-instructing learner will attempt to reconcile them.

A good example of this type of strategy can be seen in the case of Leigh, a graduate student in the field of adult education. Leigh is interested in how adults learn, and so she is studying theories of learning proposed by researchers in adult education and in psychology. The focus of the former is on adults, while the focus of the latter is on learning. Thus, Leigh asks questions about each new theory she encounters as to how it relates to what she knows about others she has studied and to what she knows about her own learning as an adult. By using such a strategy, she enhances the relevance of the new material she studies.

Affective Strategies to Heighten Confidence

Confidence is shown by the learner's *belief* that a given learning goal may be accomplished, which leads to persistence in the task. Certainly, positive self-talk, as described earlier, can be a factor in the learner's maintaining confidence. But another factor shown to influence confidence negatively is learner anxiety, or fear of doing poorly on tests, projects, or other assignments. Unfortunately, the proverbial vicious circle can ensue when anxiety leads to decreased motivation, which leads to poor performance, which in turn confirms students' fears and intensifies their anxiety.

Students may use various approaches to overcome debilitating anxiety, including relaxation techniques, positive self-talk, and test-taking techniques. The latter can be particularly effective in helping students to budget their time appropriately during a learning or test-taking situation.

Finally, self-instructing students may heighten confidence by employing the general strategy of breaking the overall learning task into manageable parts. In this way, they may successfully complete each subtask and gain confidence for achieving the larger goal.

Affective Strategies to Promote Satisfaction

When self-instructing learners employ self-checks to supply those events of instruction called elicit performance and provide feedback, they use a strategy that simultaneously promotes satisfaction. In other words, they confirm the expectancy with which they began the learning task, and this constitutes a satisfying result.

Learners may also use reinforcement strategies to good effect in maintaining motivation. For example, you may decide that, for 3 hours in the library researching an independent project, you will reward yourself with a quiet walk through the woods, or a half-hour's break listening to your favorite records. In this way, you may look forward to the prize you have promised yourself and thus stay motivated at your learning task.

Summary

In this section, we have discussed affective strategies that self-instructing learners may use to maintain their motivation throughout a learning task. Typically, learners incorporate such strategies as these into the general plan for approaching a learning goal. Obviously, a highly motivated learner will have little need for many of the motivational strategies we discussed, or may employ some of them automatically. But a skilled self-learner will recognize when additional motivational support may be necessary and will strive to provide it during the learning process.

ACQUISITION OF LEARNER STRATEGIES

The ways in which students acquire learner strategies, and thus how such strategies may be taught to learners, depends on a number of factors.

1. Make a list of motivational strategies you commonly employ as a learner to (a) keep yourself on task (maintain attention), (b) enhance the relevance of a learning goal to you, (c) improve your confidence about learning, and (d) enhance your satisfaction in learning. Compare your list to that of another student, and discuss your differences. Then discuss what aspects about a learning goal or task would cause you to employ different strategies.

2. Suppose, as a teacher, you noticed a student in your class who appeared to lack confidence even though he or she had the requisite skills to accomplish any task you assigned. What strategies might you teach this student to overcome the problem? Explain why.

First, the degree of simplicity or complexity of a strategy will determine whether a learner can acquire it just by being told or by being given opportunities to practice it. Second, the age of the learner has some bearing on strategy use, because young learners may not possess the metacognitive knowledge necessary for determining when to use certain strategies. Young children, for example, may know a particular strategy but not use it unless reminded. In addition, whether a strategy is general or specific affects its acquisition and use. This particularly refers to problem-solving strategies. That is, a domain-specific strategy such as that used to solve algebraic word problems would be acquired under different conditions than a general strategy such as isolating a factor in a problem and attempting to eliminate it.

Finally, the prior knowledge a learner possesses in a given domain will influence what strategies can be acquired and used. Novices tend to use more general strategies because they do not have the content knowledge to have acquired domain-specific strategies. It is also true that younger learners will not have acquired the body of knowledge possessed by older learners, which means that the strategies they can use will be less complex. Let us examine each of these factors in somewhat more detail.

Simple vs. Complex Task Strategies

Some strategies are so simple that learners acquire them easily by being told what they are. You have probably experienced the phenomenon of having someone tell you or show you a new approach to a particular kind of problem and thinking, "Why didn't I think of that?" Then, forever after, you employ the strategy because it makes the task easier. Examples of simple strategies appear in most subject domains. They include such things as: reading the headings or first sentences in each paragraph to get an overview of what a text is about; breaking a large learning task into parts and learning these one by one; and grouping pieces that are alike when constructing something from a kit.

More complex or involved strategies may require extensive practice on the part of the learner to acquire them effectively. The imagery mnemonic-keyword method (described in Chapter 5), is an example of this type of strategy. The learner can be told how to use the keyword method in learning foreign language vocabulary words, for example, but then needs to have numerous opportunities to practice it. The practice helps to make some of the steps of the strategy automatic, so that when learners again encounter foreign words to learn, they are likely to use the strategy with great facility.

Retrieval strategies such as notetaking also require extensive practice for learners to acquire and use effectively. Many systems of notetaking exist, and all are more effective for enhancing retrieval than leaving learners to their own devices. For a learner to acquire one of these systems, however, direct instruction on the system and practice in using it are essential.

Age-dependent Strategy Use

According to Derry and Murphy (1986), "Students of nearly any age and ability can be induced to rehearse, take notes, outline, and so forth" (p. 10). In other words, learners representing a wide range of ages are capable of learning many types of strategies. Where learners differ, then, is in whether they actually use the strategies they know. And in this respect, a developmental trend has been observed: older learners tend to use strategies more often and more effectively than younger learners. Studies contrasting the behavior of disabled and normal children have also found that disabled learners are less efficient and less "planful" (Torgesen, 1977).

This means, then, that what learners know about how and when to employ strategies—their metacognition—may be related to their age and experience. Younger, less experienced learners are less likely to approach a learning task with a general plan. And they are less likely to monitor their own activities during the learning process. This is not to say they cannot do these things, simply that they do not. Future research holds the key to determining how easily young learners may be taught metacognitive knowledge (Pressley et al., 1984).

Specific vs. General Problem-Solving Strategies

Problem-solving strategies in general include those techniques that help to guide learners toward a solution to some problem. The problem-solving process involves, first, understanding the problem, then searching for a way to solve it, and finally implementing the procedures to solve it that were discovered in the search (Gick, 1986). Thus, learners may employ strategies to help decode the problem as well as to help solve it. And typically, the more learners know about the subject domain of the problem, the more likely they are to employ *domain-specific* strategies. Conversely, the less experience or knowledge learners have of the subject, the more likely they are to use *general* strategies.

To understand this distinction better, consider the example of an experienced versus a resident physician diagnosing a patient's symptoms. Because the experienced doctor has seen the same symptoms numerous times, there may be immediate recognition of the cause and reasonable certainty of the correctness of the diagnosis. The resident doctor, on the other hand, is more likely to proceed with an analysis of each symptom, checking it against a variety of ailments known to cause such a symptom. When the best fit of observed symptoms is reached with the disease known to cause such symptoms, this diagnosis is selected.

The experienced physician's strategy was *schema-driven,* or domain-specific. That is, a schema is relied on to diagnose the disease, a schema that had been built by prior knowledge and experience. The resident physician's strategy was more general, *search-based,* searching for and analyzing alternative solutions before choosing one. You can see that this search strategy could be applicable to a wide variety of problem types, and this is the reason for its being called general in nature.

Content-specific strategies are acquired as the learner gains more knowledge of the content field and solves many problems of the same type in similar contexts. More general strategies appear to be acquired when the learner solves problems in a wide range of contexts. In other words, the learner acquires the ability to *generalize* or *transfer* a strategy from one situation to another. Both types of strategies are important for problem solving and hold quite different implications for teaching.

IMPLICATIONS FOR TEACHING LEARNER STRATEGIES

Programs exist that are designed to teach learner strategies outside of the student's regular school curriculum (e.g., McCombs, 1981–1982; Weinstein, 1982). These courses have typically been aimed at older students who lack the study skills to be successful in an academic program. And they treat academic subject matter as incidental practice material. The approach exemplified by these programs has been termed the *detached strategies training approach.*

Detached strategies training programs have seen some modest success in helping students to become better learners. The most successful of these teach students about cognition and about the regulation of cognition (McKeachie, Pintrich, & Lin, 1985). In these programs, students learn a variety of strategies and how these strategies relate to task demands. They also learn how to regulate their cognition, that is, how to select and use strategies to maximize their own learning.

One of the recurrent problems with detached strategies training programs, however, pertains to their inability to supply *long-term varied practice* in strategy formulation and use. Students may learn some useful strategies, but they typically do not get enough experience in the application of these strategies. They may learn general strategies, but they typically cannot learn very specific strategies because no new subject matter content is taught. You might think of this problem as, "Students must learn *some stuff* before they can learn *to think about* that stuff!"

Another example of a detached strategies training program illustrates this point very well. The program, Feuerstein's instrumental enrichment (FIE) (Feuerstein, Rand, Hoffman, & Miller, 1980), was designed initially for children who exhibited impulsive problem-solving behavior. It followed similar methods to those described earlier in that it attempted not only to teach children particular strategies but also to increase their awareness of their own thinking. The effectiveness of this program, however, was found to depend on three critical factors: (1) instructors received at least 1 week of training in the method; (2) students participated in the program for 80 hours or more over a 1- to 2-year period; and (3) the strategies were taught in conjunction with subject matter of interest and importance to students (Savell, Twohig, & Rachford, 1986).

The alternative to detached strategies training is *embedded strategies training*, which means that instruction and extended practice in the use of strategies are provided within the context of existing curricula (Jones et al., 1985; Campione & Armbruster, 1985). This approach has the advantage of being easy to implement without extensive in-service training for teachers. Within their own classes, then, teachers can teach content-specific strategies, provide study questions and activities that require particular thinking processes, and employ study prompts, or reminders to students to use particular processing strategies.

To capture the benefits of both approaches to teaching strategies— detached and embedded—Derry and Murphy (1986) propose a combined approach, which they describe as follows:

> In our model school, a middle school perhaps, the first 2 weeks of each year are devoted to the training of learning skills. Learning strategies training includes instructional units on the following topics: time management, mood management, study reading, memorization skills, and problem-solving techniques. Although different teachers are responsible for differ-

ent topics, their efforts are coordinated. One form of coordination is through the use of a common planning model, or metastrategy, called the Four C's Learning Plan. The four C's are as follows: clarify the learning situation; come up with a plan; carry out the plan; and check your results. Thus language arts teachers explain how reading and memorization tactics fit into the four C's, while math teachers explain problem-solving, and physical education teachers explain mood control tactics using the same framework. (p. 18)

You can see in this description the deliberate use of the type of general plan for employing strategies that we described earlier. Calling students' attention to this plan facilitates their metacognitive awareness and helps them to become more planful in learning.

Summary: Recommendations for Teaching Learner Strategies

Teachers can do a great deal to promote students' acquisition of effective and useful processing and motivational strategies. Beginning in the primary grades, they may systematically provide the experiences necessary for students to become independent learners. How may teachers best do this? Some general principles are as follows.

Match strategies to the processing requirements of the learning task. Throughout this chapter (and this book), we have emphasized the need to provide appropriate conditions of learning to activate particular learning processes and to support particular learning outcomes. In the case of learner strategies, teachers can direct students to use those strategies shown to influence a given process when that process is required for learning. That is, teachers can teach, and direct students to use, attention or encoding strategies at the time the processes of attention or encoding are prominent in the learning act. Also, the emphasis on type of strategy to use at any given time depends on the nature of the desired learning outcome.

Provide learner strategies instruction consistent with the students' current knowledge and skill level. Simple task strategies may be taught to very young learners, while more complex strategies should be reserved for older, more experienced learners. Similarly, teaching general problem-solving strategies is appropriate in the beginning stages of instruction, when learners have not yet acquired much content knowledge. As students learn more about a topic, they are able to tackle more content-specific problem-solving strategies.

Arrange for extensive practice in strategy use. Once students have been told or shown how to use a given strategy, they must have numerous opportunities to practice it. When a domain-specific strategy has been taught, students should be asked to solve many problems of the same type. To enhance the transferability of general strategies, however, students should be required to solve problems in a wide range of contexts. It is in teaching these general strategies that a group of teachers may coordinate their efforts, as Derry and Murphy (1986) describe. In other words, an English teacher may illustrate how a given strategy applies to reading for comprehension, while a math teacher illustrates the use of the same strategy with arithmetic word problems. Strategy practice in all domains helps to ensure the development of self-regulated learning.

Prompt students, as necessary, to use strategies. The intent of prompting is to encourage students to recall and practice previously acquired learner strategies. Prompts may be an integral part of the instructional materials, as in adjunct questions that require particular thinking processes. Or they may be inserted at appropriate points in instruction as directions to the student, brief reminders to use certain strategies. Extensive prompting is likely to be required with younger learners and with learners who have demonstrated deficiencies in learning skills. As learners acquire a repertory of strategies and begin to demonstrate independent, self-regulated learning, prompting may be phased out.

Promote metacognitive awareness in the early stages of instruction. Learners are more effective at self-instruction when they are aware of their own thinking processes and how to select and use the strategies most appropriate to the learning goal. They may also be more highly motivated to learn and use a given strategy if they are aware of how it might be useful to them. This argues for teaching students how to regulate strategies as well as how to do them.

While conscious awareness of strategies is useful when they are first being learned and applied, a desirable long-range goal is for the strategies, and the regulation of them, to become automatic. When strategies are automatic, learners are free to devote their attention to the processing of content. In order to promote automaticity, teachers need follow only those principles already discussed, namely, provide extensive practice and prompt at necessary (Derry & Murphy, 1986).

CONCLUSION

Improvement of learning ability is not only an important goal for education, it is a viable one. We have discussed in this chapter a variety of techniques that learners can employ to enhance their own internal processing, as well as manage their own motivation, during learning. Acquisition of these strategies, which characterize the independent thinker or self-learner, is a matter of learning what to do, why to do it, and when to do it.

As we have shown, *what* to do depends on the processing requirements of the learning goal, and, in the case of motivation, what motivational problems the learner seeks to avoid or overcome. *Why* and *when* to use a strategy are aspects of metacognition, or the learners' awareness of their own thinking processes and the perceived utility of the strategy.

In order to teach learner strategies most effectively, then, or to arrange conditions that will best promote their development, teachers should, first, teach strategies within the context of the regular school curriculum and subject matter. With attention to task demands and learner characteristics, teachers may provide direct instruction, followed by extensive practice, in both specific and general strategies. Finally, providing information about strategy use and utility, and furnishing prompts to use particular strategies, can help to guarantee the development of desirable self-learning skills.

Summary Exercise

1. Observe an experienced, or "master," teacher in your field.
   a. What processing or motivational strategies does this teacher provide as opportunities for learning? How is this accomplished?
   b. Make a list of processing and/or motivational strategies that could be appropriately taught in this class, being sure to identify each type of strategy.
   c. Using the recommendations described in this chapter, describe how you might incorporate, into this class, specific instruction and practice on one or more strategies.
2. In the event that observation of a practicing teacher is not possible, or in addition to an observation, generate a plan for how you might incorporate instruction on learning and motivational strategies in your own instruction.

GENERAL REFERENCES

Cognitive Strategies

Gagné, R. M. (1985). *The conditions of learning,* 4th ed. New York: Holt, Rinehart and Winston.

Pressley, M, & Levin, J. R. (1983). *Cognitive strategy research: Educational applications.* New York: Springer-Verlag.

Pressley, M., & Levin, J. R. (1983). *Cognitive strategy research: Psychological foundations.* New York: Springer-Verlag.

Learning Strategies

Levin, J. R., & Pressley, M. (Eds). (1986). Special issue: Learning strategies. *Educational Psychologist, 21* (1 & 2).

Segal, J. R., Chipman, S. F., & Glaser, R. (1985). *Thinking and learning skills: Relating instruction to research,* Vol. 1. Hillsdale, NJ: Erlbaum.

The Teaching of Learning Strategies

Derry, S. J., & Murphy, D. A. (1986). Designing systems that train learning ability: From theory to practice. *Review of Educational Research, 56*(1), 1–39.

Weinstein, C. E., & Mayer, R. E. (1985). The teaching of learning strategies. In M. C. Wittrock (Ed.), *Handbook of research on teaching,* 3rd ed. New York: Macmillan.

EIGHT
DELIVERING INSTRUCTION

Once instruction has been planned, it must be delivered to students. The teacher can choose many ways to deliver instruction, and these may be combined to form a variety of patterns of external stimulation to the learner. The teacher's voice is a common mode for delivering meaningful communications, as is the printed presentation of text in a pamphlet or textbook. In addition, there are actual objects such as clocks, blocks, beads, rabbits; models like those of the solar system and the human skeleton; pictures and diagrams; pictures showing motion via film or television; and a variety of sound-producing devices. Any and all of these sources of stimulation may be woven into a great variety of combinations to perform the instructional functions discussed in Chapter 6. Technological advances have also made it possible to combine many of these resources in the delivery of instruction via computers and videodiscs.

The selection, orchestration, and delivery of stimulation by means of these various sources comprise a large portion of the decisions the teacher must make every day. Sometimes, the selection made is a critical one. For example, in learning to understand spoken French, the student must be presented with oral samples of French; a printed representation of such speech simply will not suffice. On other occasions, the decision is not so critical; for example, a suitably prepared student may learn a new fact equally well by hearing it spoken or by reading it in a text. The ultimate guide to decisions about the sources of instructional stimulation is the learning objective. The instructional event *presenting the stimulus* must of course incorporate the essential stimulation that is to cue the student's performance.

Another important area of decision making for the teacher is the matching of instructional events to the *numbers* of students they are intended to influence. There are striking individual differences among students and consequent differences in the effectiveness of various kinds of external stimulation. Assuming that the teacher is responsible for the instruction of twenty-five to forty students, there are many ways of arranging these students for purposes of delivering instruction. They can, of course, be treated as a total group; they can be arranged in several smaller groups; or they can work in twos or threes, as is common in doing science activities. Moreover, a certain portion of student instruction, which may be more or less extensive, is delivered to the *individual*. A variety of individual instruction of noteworthy educational significance is the one-to-one delivery called *tutoring*.

In this chapter we shall attempt to describe the bases for teacher decisions about ways of delivering instruction. Keeping in mind the available sources of stimulation, we will examine a variety of ways for arranging groups of students, or individual students, so that they may effectively receive and profit from instruction. Thus, we shall need to consider how the events of instruction can best be delivered and what the limitations on their delivery are for groups of class size, for small interacting groups within the class settings, and for the individual student in both self-instruction and tutoring.

INSTRUCTION IN THE CLASS

Modern school classrooms are typically quite flexible in permitting various arrangements of students into large and small groups and even for allowing individual work by students outside any group. The days of fixed seating of students in classrooms are long gone, and the availability of movable furniture, modular units, screens, and other equipment of this nature make possible many kinds of student groupings.

Although the frequency of class instruction has undoubtedly diminished, there are still many occasions in the school on which this size of student group is given instruction. What kinds of instruction can be most effectively conducted with groups of class size? How can the necessary instructional events be delivered to such groups? What limitations does this size of student group impose on instructional effectiveness?

Instructional Events in the Class Setting

Perhaps the most obvious characteristic of any class is that it is composed of individuals. The differences in performance—and in capability of performance—that these individuals display are large. There are differences among individuals that can scarcely be lessened, regardless of how effective instruction may be in attaining commonly shared goals. Of at least equal importance are the individual differences in the capabilities that different learners bring to a common learning task—differences in their *entering capabilities*. These latter characteristics constitute the raw material with which instruction must work.

As you may recall from any class in which you were a member, what the individual learners bring to a new learning task can have considerable effect on the instruction delivered to a class. Some class members are bound to have greater amounts of information than do others, on any particular subject. Students exhibit differences in entering capabilities consisting of intellectual skills and verbal information. Quite significantly, members of a class are likely to vary with regard to the cognitive strategies they possess and employ in learning, as we have seen in Chapter 7. Naturally, the attitudes held by students will differ among individuals, and these too will influence the ways in which instruction is presented.

How can instruction in a class setting deal with individual differences in what students bring to the learning activity? Are there advantages, and also limitations, to be expected of instruction in the class setting? These questions may now be considered in terms of the events of instruction described in Chapter 6. Assuming that attention has been gained, a teacher's initial task is that of communicating the objective—that is, ensuring that students know what they will be able to do once they have learned. Involved in this event are activities that arouse and sustain the motivation that relates to the learning task. The decisions to be made by the teacher are based on estimates of such matters as *what will appeal* to all the members of the class and what will *hold their interest*. Arranging these events may be readily accomplished for students whose family backgrounds are relatively homogeneous. However, they demand great ingenuity when students exhibit a wide range of backgrounds. Of course, if the teacher were acting as a tutor for a single student, estimates about that student's interests could become more exact. In any case, they require that the teacher be well acquainted with members of the class as individuals.

Stimulating recall: providing learning guidance. These instructional events make great demands on a teacher's skill. They are sometimes difficult to accomplish efficiently, because of the individual differences in entering capabilities of students. Suppose, for example, the lesson objective is "using the objective case of pronouns that are objects of prepositions" (for *her*, about *him*, between *us*, and so forth). The teacher may begin by asking students to recall one or more important prerequisites, for example, what a preposition is, what pronouns are in the objective case, and so on. The difficulty lies in assuring that all members of the class have in fact retrieved these capabilities from their memories. By the time the next learning event occurs, a few will not have done so; many will; and some may become inattentive because it takes so long for the recall performance of other students to occur.

The next event, guiding the learning, is also influenced by the fact of individual differences. If the method of "discovery learning" is to be used, the teacher might present several examples ("He sits next to *her;* she stands between *them*," and the like) and ask that the rule be stated. How many students would be able to do this? The likelihood is that a fair proportion would not. Alternatively, the teacher might proceed with this event by communicating the rule "When pronouns are objects of prepositions, they are used in the objective case." Hearing this, how many students could then be able to complete sentences like the following, using pronouns correctly: "It is strictly a matter between her and _____"? Perhaps a majority would, but possibly all would not.

Various means are used to overcome these difficulties of class instruction. Small groups of students may be formed whose members have mastered a common set of prerequisites, and for whom the estimates of needed recall and effective guidance can be more precisely arrived at. Different small groups may proceed to attain the same lesson objectives by spending more time recalling prerequisite skills and perhaps by receiving more detailed learning guidance, such as more hints or fuller prompts. Another widely employed method is to arrange instruction so that initial learning (of a new rule, for example) is done individually by students. Instructional material in workbooks may be used for this purpose. More frequently, students undertake individual self-instruction by studying a text for homework. A third method, also frequently used, consists in the teacher's calling for responses from members of the class who "need it most." In following such a procedure, the teacher uses knowledge of individual students to estimate which ones are most likely to need to reinstate previously learned capabilities in order to recover them, and which students are most likely to need hints or other kinds of cues to retrieval.

Eliciting performance and providing feedback.   Arranging these events for the class requires some ingenuity. A common method is for the teacher to call upon individual students. When such a procedure is used in the informal setting of the modern classroom, care should be taken to include those who do not volunteer as well as those who do; otherwise, an entire class period may be dominated by those students who learn most readily, to the detriment of others. In a class setting, it is not clear that at the time one student is responding the others are profiting much from this instructional event. Some may be; and the feedback provided by a good performance of the reciting student may constitute reinforcement for these other students. But many of the students who are not answering may not be attending to the answers given by their classmates. Haven't you sometimes "tuned out" when another student was answering a question? When this happens, the performance and its feedback will not be having their best effects.

To overcome this difficulty, teachers often turn to the written test or quiz, which requires each member of the class to respond to a common set of questions. When such tests do not depend on speed of reading or responding, they constitute a perfectly good method of eliciting student performance. But how shall feedback be given promptly? Here again, a reasonably good method can be applied in most instances—the exchange of test papers and the marking of correct and incorrect answers by fellow students.

On occasion, student performance must be elicited in forms that are longer and more elaborate than a quiz. This is particularly true when problem-solving tasks are assigned—as when students are asked to compare and contrast two forms of local government, or to compose an essay on injustice. The essay test is used for this purpose, as is the paper or project assigned as homework. Naturally, tests and assignments of this sort imply a genuine commitment on the part of the teacher to read and comment on these products or at least to assign grades to them. It is important in using these procedures that the feedback be as prompt and accurate as possible.

Enhancing retention and transfer.   Individual differences among class members again present the teacher of the class with problems in pursuing the aims of enhancing retention and promoting transfer of learning. Some students in a class may have acquired strategies of retrieval that are highly effective; others may not. Suggestions of retrieval techniques and cues (such as tables, diagrams, pictures), having been chosen to be most effective on the average, are typically given to the entire class. Their effectiveness, however, is bound to vary, owing to the idiosyncratic nature of individual memory stores. Alternatively, the teacher may urge students to "use their own schemes" for retrieval. For those students who already have efficient cognitive strategies for retrieval, this method should work very well. For those who do not, individual suggestions of remembering strategies such as those described in Chapter 7 may be valuable.

Spaced reviews of previously learned capabilities provide opportunities for processes of retrieval to be set in operation and thus constitute an important method of enhancing retention. Such reviews may be, and frequently are, conducted with an entire class. Again, in this situation, the teacher usually makes decisions about "who most needs to be called upon," when asking for responses from individual class members. Under such circumstances, some students will receive direct practice in retrieval; others may practice to themselves in anticipation of being called upon; and still others may not retrieve at all. An alternative method for review is a quiz, or test, in which all students face the necessity of retrieving by writing answers to a common set of questions.

Problem-solving tasks are often employed to promote transfer of learned capabilities to novel situations. Choosing suitable tasks requires an estimate that the component intellectual skills and information involved in problem solving are available to all members of the class. To the extent that they are unavailable to any students, both the problem-solving process and its outcome will be degraded in quality and scope. For example, a problem for a class in social studies might be one of predicting the growth of shops in a local shopping center, based upon the projected pattern of housing in the surrounding area. Reasonably original solutions to such a problem require a number of skills on the part of the students—the construction of graphs, extrapolation of trends, and the concepts of ease of transportation, population density, family income, and others. Students who have indeed attained these intellectual skills will be able to participate in the process of solving the problem in ways that are valuable for their learning. Students who have not attained these skills will, in a class situation, simply be acquiring some not very useful information by listening to other students.

The conduct of *class discussions,* another variety of problem-solving situation, is often plagued by these same difficulties. Ideally, the class discussion is an excellent way to promote transfer of learning. When members of a discussion group have available to them a common set of information and skills, they are able to display their originality of thought in a setting that provides valuable feedback from other members of the group. In such situations, reinforcement is provided for originality of thought, critical judgment, and facility in communicating ideas. Ideally, discussion is a most valuable method of instruction for a group of students. The ideal, however, is not achieved very frequently. In fact, the most frequent difficulty with discussion groups is the interjection of questions or comments that clearly indicate the absence of prerequisite knowledge and skills on the part of individual members.

Adapting Instructional Events to the Class

As this review of instructional events shows, the teacher makes a variety of decisions in adapting instructional events to the class setting. Individual differences among members of the class generate problems in selecting the means of influencing the learning process of each student. Particular attention is required by those differences in the repertory of capabilities that students bring to the learning situation, and these in turn result mainly from prior learning.

Initial events of instruction in the class, such as communicating objectives and establishing motivation, can often be readily accomplished in a common way for all members of the class. For example, the introduction to a lesson on anthropoid apes using pictures or movies is likely to arouse the interest and attention of an entire class. Subsequent events, including stimulating recall, guiding the learning, providing for retention and transfer, and eliciting the performance and furnishing feedback, are more likely to require some differentiation for various class members. The teacher must choose among various techniques in order to influence the learning of individual students. In order to deal directly with each member, the teacher may spend some time tutoring individuals or divide the class into smaller groups. Often, a common learning task is assigned for each member of the class to work on independently, in the classroom or in homework. In addition, individual assignments such as papers or projects are made to each member of a class or to small teams. It is evident that the teacher has available several ways of individualizing instruction and that these may be employed singly or in combination.

INSTRUCTION FOR THE INDIVIDUAL STUDENT

Two particular modes of instruction, emphasizing an orientation toward the individual learner, deserve separate discussion. First is the method that provides for interaction between two persons, the *tutorial* relationship. Second is the situation in which instruction is self-administered, often called *independent learning* (or *independent study*). As indicated in the previous section, both of these modes are employed with some frequency by the classroom teacher. Other instructional settings, however, may be designed to depend *primarily* on tutoring or independent learning. It will

1. Suppose you were the teacher of an English class in a school attended by students from a wide diversity of cultural backgrounds. Some of your students speak Spanish at home and are having difficulty learning English. Others speak various dialects of English, and still others are very competent speakers of English. How might you arrange for the events of instruction in order to accommodate the differing entry capabilities of your students?
2. Observe an experienced, or "master," teacher. Analyze the instructional decisions he or she makes in the classroom according to the following points.
   a. State the grade level of the class you observe and describe the general characteristics of the students.
   b. Describe the nature of the lesson being taught. Identify the type of learning outcome(s) focused on in the lesson.
   c. List the events of instruction, and describe what the teacher does to implement each in the lesson.
   d. Summarize your observations by describing what the teacher does to accommodate for learner differences and provide for individualized instruction.

therefore be worthwhile to examine the nature of instructional events for each of these additional modes, and to compare them with the events of class (or group) instruction.

The comparison of instructional events for three modes of instruction is made in Table 8.1. The column labeled *Group instruction* repeats in brief summary form the treatment of instructional events we have described for the class or group.

Tutorial Instruction

Comparisons of instructional events commonly employed in tutoring and in group instruction can be made by glancing down the center columns of Table 8.1. The tutor initiates the same kinds of instructional events as does the teacher of a group. Each event is, however, adapted to the particular needs and current learning status of the student. For example, the tutor is able to ask for recall of previously learned capabilities, which must be recovered by the particular student. Learning guidance is provided when the student obviously requires it. The student is told to use whatever cues are desired for retrieval. The student is asked to perform when ready, and immediate feedback of considerable accuracy is provided.

TABLE 8.1 Comparison of Instructional Events for Three Modes of Instruction: Group, Tutorial, and Individual Learning

INSTRUCTIONAL EVENT	GROUP INSTRUCTION	TUTORIAL INSTRUCTION	INDIVIDUAL LEARNING
Gaining attention	Teacher stimulates attention of group members	Tutor adapts stimulation to student interest	Student adopts attentional strategy
Informing learner of objective	Teacher communicates to group	Tutor assures student understanding of objective	Student confirms or selects objective
Stimulating recall	Teacher asks for recall by group members	Tutor checks recall of essential items	Student retrieves essential items
Presenting stimulus	Teacher gives emphasis to distinctive features	Tutor assures perception of features by student	Student attends to distinctive features
Guiding learning	Teacher suggests hints, organizers, cues to retrieval	Tutor provides cues, organizers, only when needed	Student adopts own encoding strategies
Eliciting performance	Teacher uses a test to assess performances of group members	Tutor asks for performance when student is ready	Student verifies own performance
Providing feedback	Teacher provides feedback, differing among students in precision	Tutor provides precise and immediate feedback	Student provides own feedback
Enhancing retention	Teacher provides retrieval cues and conducts spaced reviews	Tutor suggests student use own cues for retrieval; conducts reviews	Students supplies own retrieval cues, conducts own reviews
Promoting transfer	Teacher sets novel and varied tasks for all group members	Tutor sets transfer tasks adapted to student capabilities	Student adopts strategies of elaboration and generalization

Effects of tutoring.   Comparisons have been made of the effectiveness of tutoring and two forms of class instruction, one *conventional* and the other *mastery learning* (Bloom, 1984). Both of the latter two methods dealt with classes of thirty students, whereas tutoring was conducted one-on-one. The mastery learning system (Block & Anderson, 1975) permits students who lag behind others in their achievement of lesson objectives to take more time to "catch up," until each lesson is satisfactorily learned (that is, *mastered*). The highly important event that intervenes following the initially inadequate performance is *feedback and correction.* The slower learners are told that their performance does not meet a proper standard, are told what to do to complete their learning to the mastery level, and are then given a chance to do so. Compared with conventional instruction, mastery learning has been found to increase the performance of classes by 34 percent. (In terms of the normal curve, this is an increase of 1 S.D., or *1 sigma,* which is the way the increase is described by Bloom.)

Typical classes, according to this evidence, can substantially increase their average achievement level if the teacher follows mastery learning procedures. How do these class methods of instruction compare in effectiveness with the tutoring method? Compared with conventional instruction, student achievement under tutoring increases by *2 sigma,* or 50 percent. According to a number of studies, the key factors contributing to this improvement (in addition to corrective feedback) are the "enhancement of prerequisites" before learning begins and the provision of "cues and explanations" for the new learning (Bloom, 1984). These two phrases may be taken as names for the two instructional events: *stimulating recall of prior learning* and *providing learning guidance.* The importance of these events to the effectiveness of learning is confirmed by these results.

Notable is the fact that these particular events fall into the category of *alterable variables.* That is to say, they can be put into effect not only by a tutor, but also by the teacher of a class of students. These results make increasingly clear the factors that lead to the superiority of tutoring as an instructional method. And they show that some of these factors can readily be employed by teachers in the instruction of classes.

Student tutoring.   A valuable extension of the teacher's operation as a tutor is provided by student tutors. High school students may volunteer to tutor pupils in elementary grades; fourth graders may tutor first graders. In nongraded classrooms, it is not uncommon to find tutoring of students by their peers. Students who have recently learned new information or intellectual skills often make excellent tutors for their classmates who have not yet learned the same items. In fact, many different combinations of tutors and students have been and are continuing to be tried.

Student tutoring is frequently successful in accomplishing instruction, in improving achievement of tutors as well as their students, and in bringing about favorable changes in attitudes toward school learning (Ellson, Harris, & Barber, 1968; Johnson & Johnson, 1975). Programs of student tutoring apparently work best when lessons have been carefully preplanned and when the tutors have been trained to administer the instructional events described in Table 8.1. The needed training, however, can usually be accomplished in a few days' time. Programs of student tutoring require careful management by teachers, particularly with respect to the selection and training of tutors, the preplanning of lessons, and the monitoring of student progress. Such programs are capable of yielding substantial benefits in the promotion of school learning (Gartner, Kohler, & Riessman, 1971).

Self-Instruction

The contrast of individual learning, or self-instruction, with other modes can be seen by comparing appropriate columns of Table 8.1. As an individual learner, the student begins a learning task with preestablished motivation. The teacher may have had a good deal to do with establishing such motivation, or it may have been established long ago. The student finds and confirms the objective of the lesson in the textbook or other material being studied. Alternatively, a student may need to decide individually upon an objective.

Proceeding with the lesson, self-instructing students individually remind themselves of previously learned knowledge and skills that can be brought to bear on the new learning. These learners read, listen, and look selectively for portions of the communication that are of direct relevance. Further, they use whatever strategies may be available to encode the capability being learned, so that retrieval will be possible and easy. A student skilled in strategies for learning transfer may also be able to establish some broad generalizations of what has been learned. Self-instructing students know when the lesson's objective has been achieved. To make certain, they may set problems for themselves or rehearse answers to questions about what has been learned. These are all activities, described in detail in Chapter 7, that enable students to confirm the expectancy with which they began the learning task.

Individual learning obviously requires a great deal of the learner. To supply all of the self-instructional events that support learning throughout its course, the learner needs to acquire a number of cognitive strategies, of the sort described in Chapter 7. A young child will have learned few of these strategies and will need much help from instruction by the teacher. As experience is gained, the student will be able to provide more and more self-instruction. By the time high school is reached, motivated students will probably be able to do much learning on their own. When group classes are desirable, with aims of discussion and group problem solving, such students will enter such groups prepared with the necessary skills and knowledge. But students who are slow or less successful are the ones who particularly need the external support provided by the events of instruction. For these students, some aspects of the learning process may go smoothly while others do not. It is part of the teacher's job to find out which phases of learning are most likely to require external support and activation and which phases can be self-managed. In this way teaching can be adapted to subject matter, to age level, and ideally to the individual student.

For each of the following situations, describe how you, as the teacher, might employ *tutoring* and *self-instruction* to aid learning. There are no right or wrong answers. Rather, the scenarios may be used for class discussion.

SITUATION 1: In a ninth grade science class, students are learning about the circulatory systems of reptiles. The learning goals include identifying parts of the circulatory system (such as heart, arteries, etc.) as well as tracing blood flow through the bodies of such animals as earthworms and frogs. Available to the teacher are a variety of pictures, models, textbooks, and animals and tools for dissection.

SITUATION 2: In an elementary reading class, children are practicing picture–word matches. The class is relatively homogeneous, the teacher has available workbooks, flash cards, and computer drills.

SITUATION 3: In a junior high school social studies class, students are studying the history of their own community. As learning goals, the students are to document when the community was founded, where the settlers were from, how they made their living, what types of crops they grew, and so forth.

Systems of individualized instruction. There are several well-known systems of individualized instruction, some of which are in widespread use (Reiser, 1987). Generally, these systems are applicable to grades beyond the elementary.

The *personalized system of instruction (PSI)* permits students to proceed through assigned instructional materials at their own rate. Units of instruction consist of printed material in the form of text and a study guide. Mastery of each unit in the sequence must be demonstrated by the student before proceeding to the next unit. Quizzes are used to assess mastery of units, and these can be taken whenever the students consider themselves ready. Feedback is provided promptly by a student proctor, following the completion of each quiz. Students are individually informed about items correct and incorrect. In the latter case, students are expected to re-study and review and are permitted to take alternate versions of the quiz until they demonstrate mastery.

According to the originator of the PSI system (Keller, 1974), a number of features distinguish it from conventional class instruction. The requirement of unit mastery is perhaps the most important characteristic, along with the provision for student self-pacing. The system relies almost entirely on printed forms of instruction and places no emphasis on lectures, although these are sometimes incorporated.

Another system, applicable particularly to courses in science, is the *audio-tutorial system* (Postlethwait et al., 1972). In this approach, a course is divided into units of 1 week in length. Each unit begins with an audio tape presentation that serves to tutor the student through a sequence of learning activities. Other instruction is given along the way by printed materials, slides, and movies. At the same time (since units often partake of laboratory exercises), equipment, specimens, and models are made available to the student. It is expected that students will pace themselves in completing the activities of each unit, with help when required from a laboratory assistant. At the end of each week, students convene in small groups to engage in reviews and to take written quizzes.

Organizing Instruction to Include a Variety of Modes

School instruction normally includes all three modes of instruction we have described: (1) group, (2) tutorial, and (3) individual self-instruction. The organization of instruction into these modes varies from grade to grade. In the primary grades, there is a good deal of tutoring of individual children, but there are also many occasions for small group instruction and activities for the total class group. In the intermediate grades, tutoring by the teacher is usually done less frequently, but sometimes occurs with students who have specific difficulties. Beginning at this level, student tutoring in cooperative pairs may become an effective instructional mode (Johnson & Johnson, 1975). In the junior high school, there is increasing emphasis on self-instruction in the form of project and homework assignments. The trend is continued into the high school, where many new learning tasks are originally tackled by the student on a self-instructional basis. This is the case, for example, when students study a new homework assignment in their textbooks, when they write a composition, or when they undertake an individual-study project.

In the junior high and high school classes, instruction is often concerned with the support of the *recall* and *generalization* phases of learning. For example, suppose that students have studied (by self-instruction) a lesson on *the use of the definite article* in German. The next day's class is typically concerned with promoting retrieval of these rules by having students supply the definite article in new examples of German sentences. Transfer of learning may also be supported by conversation exercises which provide additional varieties of context for sentences using the definite article in different genders and cases.

A somewhat similar organization of instruction is to be seen in a social studies lesson on "Checks and balances in federal government." Over a period of time, a class may have studied the powers of the legislative, executive, and judicial branches of government. This study has also been divided between the self-instruction occurring in homework and the recall exercises in following class sessions. Now there comes a time of "putting things together." This may be done by means of a class discussion, led by the teacher, in which novel questions are posed and commented on by members of the class. For instance, the teacher might pose the following question: "Suppose Congress were to enact a bill to prohibit the publication of comic books; what kinds of 'checks' would there be on such legislation?" To be successful, such a discussion requires that relevant prior knowledge has been learned. Most probably, it has been acquired largely through self-instruction in homework assignments. The purpose of the discussion itself, however, is to enhance transfer of learning by engaging students in a group problem-solving situation.

Clearly, then, many kinds of instructional organization are available to classroom teachers. Varying degrees of emphasis can be placed upon the three modes of (1) group instruction, (2) tutoring, and (3) self-instruction, depending on the needs of particular circumstances. Generally, it is not desirable for teachers to attempt to force instruction into one mode at the expense of another—all three are useful. Age differences, subject matter differences, and individual student differences must all be taken into account in organizing instruction. For the skillful teacher, decisions about instructional organization should come to depend heavily upon the answers to two questions:

1. What *kind* of capability is to be learned?
2. What *kinds of support* for learning processes must be provided by instructional events?

Making instructional decisions that are soundly based on answers to these questions should be possible for readers who have studied learning in this book. Teachers can, first, classify the objectives of instruction in the *categories* of verbal information, intellectual skill, cognitive strategy, attitude, motor skill, or combinations of these. Next, it will be possible to see how these objectives are to be attained by learning—by the *processes* of expectancy through reinforcement which must occur for learning to be accomplished. Any given interval of student activity—a class period, a project, a homework assignment—can then be seen as containing *instructional events* designed to support one or more of these learning processes. At this point realistic decisions about organizing instruction become possible. For a particular student, or for the class of students, can these events best be made to happen by group instruction, by tutoring, or by self-instruction? Chances are a mixture will be chosen. The best mixture is one that is systematically organized, rather than put together at random; it is one that takes advantage of the strong features of each instructional mode.

USING AUDIO AND VISUAL MEDIA

Our introductory comments to this chapter included the idea that the delivery of instruction often involves decisions about *media*. Besides the common media for instruction (the teacher's oral delivery, the blackboard, the textbook), there are some media that are more specialized in their uses and tend also to be based on more complex hardware. *Pictures* are more or less readily available to the teacher. Some are incorporated in textbooks, others are separately obtainable or capable of being constructed. They occur also in the form of slides and filmstrips. *Pictures with motion* are seen as films and in television programs. *Audio* presentations usually accompany the visual in motion pictures and television and appear by themselves in tape players, including the useful cassette players. *Combinations* of media (print, pictures, audio messages) may be put together in various ways by various devices. For example, slide–tape and filmstrip–sound combinations are frequently used in instruction. Surely the most elaborate media combination is provided by the use of the *computer* to manage and deliver instruction.

Audio and visual media are often particularly useful to the teacher in adapting instruction to the individual needs of students. For example, in the early grades, pictures are often employed to convey meaning to children who have not yet learned to read and also to provide concrete examples of concepts and rules that are being learned. Pictures, films, and television programs can serve a similar purpose for older students or adults who have difficulty in reading. Audio presentations may also have this function. This function is in addition to their role in presenting essential kinds of stimulation, as in the fields of music and language learning. Thus, one of the important uses of media is to make possible alternate modes of communication in the delivery of instruction.

We cannot here describe in detail the kinds of audio-visual media available for instruction and their characteristic uses, strengths, and limitations. A number of texts and technical books are available on these topics, and some of them are listed at the end of this chapter. At this point, we include only a few comments on media, designed to show how they may enter into the instructional process. Decisions about the use of media must be based on what capability is being learned and how the events of instruction can best be presented when particular media are employed (Briggs & Wager, 1981; Gagné, Briggs, & Wager, 1988). The following sections illustrate these ideas with *pictures, television programs, audio cassettes,* and *computer-based instruction.*

Pictures

Pictures are commonly used as supplements to printed text. They may play a part, although not necessarily a unique one, in arousing and maintaining motivation. They may be well employed to aid selective perception of the stimulus (instructional event 4, Chapter 6) by directing attention to distinctive features. Their primary usefulness, however, occurs in the presentation of learning guidance (instructional event 5). Pictures are often excellent means of *encoding* what is to be learned, thus to assure that cues for retrieval are readily accessible. Three kinds of encoding uses for pictures are illustrated in Figure 8.1.

An obvious use of a picture is to provide an illustration of an object. The picture of the ibex serves as a coding device for many purposes for which the word "ibex" may be used in comprehending a text. The picture may be stored in the form of an image, standing in place of the defined concept "a wild goat with large curved horns." A second kind of picture is a diagram, which may be used to code an abstract concept like "focus." The student of science may readily acquire and retain "focus" by using the diagram as a code. In this case, the diagram aids in the storage and retrieval of the component concepts necessary to define the word (that is, the defined concept). Without the picture, the definition would need to be retained as a verbal statement such as "a point at which rays of light meet when refracted by a lens."

Still a third use of pictures as media for the encoding stage is shown in Figure 8.1C. Here the picture represents action, or an unfolding set

A. ACTUAL OBJECT

IBEX

B. DIAGRAM

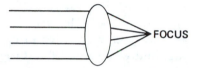

C. ACTION

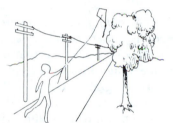

FIGURE 8.1   Three uses of pictures in the encoding phase of learning.

of events. Quite evidently a picture of this sort aids in the comprehension and storage of a text like the following: "Donald had to run to keep the string from touching the branches of the tree. When gusts of wind came along, there was a chance for the kite to dive onto the wires, or to get entangled with a pole." Research studies have shown the particular effectiveness of pictures in performing a coding function of this sort (Bransford & Johnson, 1972; Paivio, 1971).

Television Programs

The motion pictures which may be shown via televison programs have a number of potential advantages as media for instruction. Viewing television appears to be an activity that is inherently motivating. For children or adults, the desire to see events unfolding before their eyes is strong. It is a well-known fact that nearly everyone has difficulty not looking at television and also that so long as new scenes or programs are made to appear, few people get tired of watching. The motivational features of television programs, therefore, are widely acknowledged. Some additional characteristics of television need to be considered pertaining to its use in instruction.

Gaining and maintaining attention.   The motion and abrupt changes that may be introduced in television programs are of particular use in gaining and controlling attention. This feature is used to good advantage in the series of television programs called *Sesame Street.* Each program consists of a series of brief scenes, varied in content, and many abrupt changes occur between scenes as well as within them. These techniques are highly effective in capturing and holding the attention of young children (Lesser, 1974). Programs for older students and adults use similar techniques for controlling attention, although the brevity of scenes and the frequency of abrupt changes do not need to be as extreme.

Learning guidance.   Television programs are able to perform the encoding functions described in Chapter 5 with great effectiveness. They can show pictures of actual objects of infinite variety and thus convey the meanings of new concepts in concrete form. They can display many kinds of diagrams, including those that have moving parts. And of course they have great versatility in depicting action sequences of real or dramatized events, thus providing vivid scenes for the encoding (and elaboration) of concepts and rules that are to be learned (Reiser & Gagné, 1983).

The learning of organized verbal information can also be greatly aided by television presentation. One of the main functions of the moving pictures is that of *elaboration*—providing a meaningful context to which the learner can relate new information. Pictorial presentations can display a broad sweep of events in a relatively short space of time, and thus save the student time in developing a schema for newly acquired information.

One of the most striking ways in which television programs can contribute to instruction is in the establishment and modification of attitudes. In this case, the encoding function is associated with the effect of using human models. Heroes and heroines of fiction, personages of history, and political or sports figures—all can be presented in realistic form by television programs. Whoever is selected as a model, that person can be seen making the choice of personal action that is to be modeled by the learner. Thus, the television program enormously extends the range of possible human models that can be employed to appeal to a variety of students.

Performance and feedback. The chief limitations of the television medium lie in its inability to require performance of the learner and to respond to this performance with feedback. Watching television may, after all, be a passive kind of activity. One cannot be certain that the learner has learned to *use* the new concept he saw on the screen. In addition, the television picture cannot make individual corrections or confirmations of the learner's performance. *Sesame Street* makes an attempt to overcome these limitations, in effect, by encouraging the young viewer to "talk back" to the screen. Thus, when children are learning a sequence of digits ("one, two, three," and so forth), they are encouraged to say them aloud and to anticipate the program voice by completing the series before being told. Other techniques of a similar sort are used to get children to perform and then to provide feedback for their performance. These techniques are ingenious, and they work at least part of the time.

For older students, the performance and feedback phases of instruction cannot be so easily taken care of by "talking back" procedures. Printed materials containing blanks to be filled in by the student, in response to questions or problems displayed on the television screen, are sometimes used with good effect.

Audio Tape Cassettes

The tape cassette that delivers audio messages is a highly convenient and relatively inexpensive medium. Audio cassettes are of particular usefulness in providing individualized instruction. Tape players can readily be operated by the individual student and even by young children. Not only is a considerable variety of prerecorded tapes available, but also new messages may easily be recorded to fill different instructional purposes.

It is not clear that auditory messages have a particularly valuable function in controlling attention, although this possibility should not be overlooked. When auditory instructions are interspersed with printed text, they may be useful in directing attention and in promoting selective perception by emphasizing features of the message.

Audio tapes can be particularly useful in various phases of the instructional process to communicate to learners who are too young to read, or who are not good readers. For example, children who are learning to read can in effect be "read to" by an audio tape. While hearing the story on tape, they can read along in the text and thereby confirm or correct their own attempts at identifying words. For older students who are slow readers, audio tapes are sometimes used to good advantage in communicating lesson objectives, stimulating recall, and informing students about activities to be done. Naturally, auditory messages and sounds are also of particular usefulness when the learning to be done requires this mode of communication—as, for example, with instruction in music or foreign languages.

Computer-Based Instruction

Many of the instructional functions performed by other media can be combined by the use of a computer along with suitable programs for instruction. On the whole, the computer is by far the most versatile kind of equipment for instruction (Wager & Gagné, 1987).

Gaining and maintaining attention.   Since the contents of computer-based instruction are presented on a screen, most of the features of visual displays available to television may be employed. The computer display may introduce sudden stimulus changes of many sorts, capable of commanding attention. The techniques of rapidly changing figures, unusual transformations of shapes, and other screen configurations offer many possibilities for gaining and holding attention.

Presenting the stimulus.   Again in the case of this instructional event, the computer display may be used to present many kinds of visual stimuli, including both print and outlined figures. Synthetic speech may also be presented, as in a lesson asking students to identify in print (on the screen) the spoken sound of a syllable like "rom." The computer displays may be employed in the presentation of basic skills instruction in reading, writing, and arithmetic.

Still another kind of stimulus presentation possible to the computer is *simulation.* For example, problems in physical motion may be displayed in dynamic form, so that the learner can observe directly what happens to a frictionless object on an inclined plane, or how ice crystals form in storm clouds. When computer displays are used to present simulations, students may have opportunities to practice solving a great many kinds of problems, in virtually any content area.

Providing learning guidance.   Computer-based instruction is readily able to provide several kinds of learning guidance for the learning of intellectual skills and verbal information. For example, a complex procedure such as finding a fault in an electric circuit may be displayed as a diagram. Tables and graphs may be shown to illustrate relationships such as the supply of goods and their cost, or the acidity of soil and the growth of plants. Pictures of concrete objects may be outlined and used by the learner as memorable images. An abstract idea like *transport,* for example, might be recalled by means of images connecting the concrete concepts *train* and *port.*

When used for establishing attitudes, computer-based instruction has occasion to use drawings of human or animal figures as human models. These figures represent human beings or human qualities, and come to relate the choice of personal action that indicates the presence of the attitude. In subsequent periods of instruction or practice, these figures can be *embedded* in the presentation, so that they serve as reminders that help to maintain the attitude (Derry & Murphy, 1986). Thus, a figure representing the attitude of carefulness in the reading of printed text (such as an owl) might be used initially to establish the attitude and occur later as an embedded figure when learning is required from newly introduced text.

Responding and feedback.   Instruction via computer can readily incorporate provision for learner responding and feedback appropriate to that response. In other words, the feedback provided in well-designed computer instruction is precise in relation to the correctness or degree of correctness of the learner's response. For this reason in particular, computer-based instruction is well suited for the learning of intellectual skills. If a concept is being acquired, feedback can include information about correct examples and about closely similar examples that are incorrect. The application of rules, too, can be practiced in varieties of examples that follow learner responses with immediate feedback.

In the practice of basic skills, computers have still another advantage besides their precision in indicating response correctness. This resides in the fact that computers can give feedback to the *quickness* of the learner's response. In view of the desirability of attaining automaticity in certain basic skills (cf. Bloom, 1986; Gagné, 1983), measuring learners' speed of response to practice examples is likely to have great usefulness in performance assessment: for example, the quickness with which learners can supply missing verbs in sentences like the following: Every adult American citizen h_____ the right to vote. Or, how quickly can the learner complete subtractions such as 42 minus 17, or -27 minus -4? Quickness of response is one indicator of the skill automaticity that is of great significance for using intellectual skills as prerequisites for additional learning and problem solving.

For a subject or class you might someday teach, generate examples of how you might incorporate each of the following in your instruction. For each example, be sure to identify which events of instruction would be the most effectively implemented for the goal you describe.

PICTURES:

TELEVISION:

AUDIO TAPES:

COMPUTER:

SOME SUMMARIZING COMMENTS

Teachers have many decisions to make in arranging for the *delivery* of instruction, over and above those that may be made when it is originally designed. Typically, instruction is delivered in three different modes—as group instruction, by tutoring, or by student self-instruction. These modes are not entirely distinct from each other, however. They are simply convenient ways of thinking about the various forms that instruction may take. Typically, the teacher who is responsible for a class of twenty-five to thirty students uses all these modes, and mixtures of them, at various times and for various purposes.

A second set of choices to be made in the delivery of instruction concerns the audio and visual media to be used. Simple forms of media like the chalkboard and the printed text are well known. Other media use materials and hardware that are more or less complex, ranging from the still picture to the computer. Media choices are best based upon the particular contributions that can be made to instruction by various audio and visual devices.

Both kinds of decisions—those for instructional mode and for audio-visual media—require careful consideration of two questions:

1. What kind of capability is to be learned?
2. How can the various events for instruction best be made to occur?

Absolute rules for choosing modes of instruction and media in light of these questions are difficult to formulate. Often, the choices that are made represent genuine compromises with ideal conditions. What will be of greatest help is knowing that effective learning conditions are *different* for intellectual skills, information, cognitive strategies, attitudes, and motor skills. Each kind of learning outcome must be considered as a separate type of problem to be solved. Each requires somewhat different arrangements of the events of instruction, even though these events follow a common pattern beginning with an attention-gaining event and ending with feedback. In consequence, the choices of instructional modes and media are likewise found to be different for each purpose. Some learning is almost bound to occur, regardless of the teacher's decisions. The teacher will be concerned to ask, "Why not make the instruction as good as possible?"

Summary Exercise

Use the following questions to help you plan a lesson on a topic you expect to teach. In selecting your topic, you might choose to reorganize and revise some instruction you have already delivered at one time, or you may choose to design an entirely new lesson.

1. What is the overall goal of the lesson?
2. Who are the students to whom this lesson is to be taught? (grade level, potential number of students, other characteristics)
3. What specific *objectives* make up this overall goal? List each one in terms of the *capability* that is to be acquired. Then identify what kind of learning outcome each is (e.g., verbal information, intellectual skill, etc.).
4. Identify for each objective what specific learning conditions should be used in the lesson.
5. For each objective, identify how the events of instruction could be implemented.
6. Using the results of 4 and 5, decide what instructional mode might be best for delivering each objective. (class instruction, tutorial, self-instruction, or any combination)
7. On the basis of the decisions made in 4, 5, and 6, indicate how any audiovisual media might be effectively incorporated to provide for various events of instruction.

GENERAL REFERENCES

Teaching Modes

Gagné, R. M. (1985). *The conditions of learning,* 4th ed. New York: Holt, Rinehart and Winston.
Joyce, B., & Weil, M. (1972). *Models of teaching.* Englewood Cliffs, NJ: Prentice Hall.
Postlethwait, S. N., Novak, J., & Murray, H. T., Jr. (1972). *The audio-tutorial approach to learning,* 3rd ed. Minneapolis: Burgess.
Reigeluth, C. M. (Eds.) (1983). *Instructional-design theories and models.* Hillsdale, NJ: Erlbaum.

Audiovisual Media

Knirk, F. G., & Gustafson, K. L. (1986). *Instructional technology: A systematic approach to education.* New York: Holt, Rinehart and Winston.
Reiser, R. A., & Gagné, R. M. (1983). *Selecting media for instruction.* Englewood Cliffs, NJ: Educational Technology.
Romiszowski, A. J. (1974). *The selection and use of instructional media.* London: Kegan Paul.
Salomon, G. (1981). *Communication and education: Social and psychological interactions.* Beverly Hills, CA: Sage.
Schramm, W. (1977). *Big media, little media.* Beverly Hills, CA: Sage.

REFERENCES

Adams, J. A. (1967). *Human memory.* New York: McGraw-Hill.

Anderson, J. R. (1985). *Cognitive psychology and its implications,* 2nd ed. San Francisco: Freeman.

Anderson, J. R., & Bower, G. H. (1972). Recognition and retrieval processes in free recall. *Psychological Review, 79,* 97–123.

Atkinson, R. C., & Shiffrin, R. M. (1968). Human memory: A proposed system and its control processes. In K. W. Spence & J. T. Spence (Eds.), *The psychology of learning and motivation,* Vol. 2. New York: Academic Press.

Ausubel, D. P. (1968). *Educational psychology: A cognitive view.* New York: Holt, Rinehart and Winston.

Ausubel, D. P., & Fitzgerald, D. (1961). The role of discriminability in meaningful verbal learning and retention. *Journal of Educational Psychology, 52,* 266–274.

Bandura A. (1969). *Principles of behavior modification.* New York: Holt, Rinehart and Winston.

Bandura A. (1971). Vicarious and self-reinforcement processes. In R. Glaser (Ed.), *The nature of reinforcement.* New York: Academic Press.

Bandura A. (1977). Self-efficacy: Toward a unifying theory of behavioral change. *Psychological Review, 84,* 191–215.

Bellezza, F. S. (1981). Mnemonic devices: Classification, characteristics, and criteria. *Review of Educational Research, 51,* 247–275.

Berlyne, D. E. (1965). *Structure and direction in thinking.* New York: Wiley.

Block, J. H., & Anderson, L. W. (1975). *Mastery learning in classroom instruction.* New York: Macmillan.

Bloom, B. S. (1984, June). The 2-sigma problem: The search for methods of group instruction as effective as one-to-one tutoring. *Educational Researcher,* 4–15.

Bloom, B. S. (1986, February). "The hands and feet of genius". Automaticity. *Educational Leadership,* 70–77.

Bloom, B. S., Hastings, J. T., & Madaus, G. F. (1971). *Handbook on formative and summative evaluation of student learning.* New York: McGraw-Hill.

Bower, G. H., & Hilgard, E. R. (1981). *Theories of learning,* 5th ed. Englewood Cliffs, NJ: Prentice Hall.

Bransford, J. D. (1979). *Human cognition.* Belmont, CA: Wadsworth.

Bransford, J. D., & Johnson, M. K. (1972). Contextual prerequisites for understanding: Some investigations of comprehension and recall. *Journal of Verbal Learning and Verbal Behavior, 11,* 717–726.

Briggs, L. J. (Ed.). (1977). *Instructional design: Principles and applications.* Englewood Cliffs, NJ: Educational Technology.

Briggs, L. J., & Wager, W. W. (1981). *Handbook of procedures for the design of instruction.* Englewood Cliffs, NJ: Educational Technology.

Brown, A. L. (1980). Metacognitive development and reading. In R. J. Spiro, B. C. Bruce, & W. F. Brewer (Eds.), *Theoretical issues in reading comprehension.* Hillsdale, NJ: Erlbaum.

Brown, A. L., & Smiley, S. S. (1977). Rating the importance of structural units of prose passages: A problem of metacognitive development. *Child Development, 48,* 1–8.

Bruner, J. S. (1966). *Toward a theory of instruction.* Cambridge: Harvard University Press.

Bruner, J. S. (1971). *The relevance of education.* New York: Norton.

Campione, J. C., & Armbruster, B. (1985). Acquiring information from texts: An analysis of four approaches. In J. W. Segal, S. Chipman, & R. Glaser (Eds.), *Thinking and learning skills,* Vol 1. Hillsdale, NJ: Erlbaum.

Carmichael, L., Hogan, H. F., & Walter, A. A. (1932). An experimental study of the effect of language on the reproduction of visually perceived form. *Journal of Experimental Psychology, 15,* 73–86.

Carrier, C. A., & Titus, A. (1981). Effects of note-taking pretraining and test mode expectations on learning from lectures. *American Educational Research Journal, 18,* 385–397.

Conrad, R. (1964). Acoustic confusions in immediate memory. *British Journal of Psychology, 55,* 75–84.

Covington, M. V., Crutchfield, R. S., Davies, L. B., & Olton, R. M. (1972). *The productive thinking program.* Columbus, OH: Merrill.

Dansereau, D. (1985). Learning strategy research. In J. W. Segal, S. F. Chipman, & R. Glaser (Eds.), *Thinking and learning skills* (Vol. 1). Hillsdale, NJ: Erlbaum.

Derry, S. J., & Murphy, D. A. (1986). Designing systems that train learning ability: From theory to practice. *Review of Educational Research, 56*(1), 1–39.

Ellson, D. G., Barber, L., Engle, T. L., & Kampwerth, L. (1965). Programmed tutoring: A teaching aid and a research tool. *Reading Research Quarterly, 1,* 77–127.

Ellson, D. G., Harris, P., & Barber, L. (1968). A field test of programmed and directed tutoring. *Reading Research Quarterly, 3,* 307–367.

Estes, W. K. (1964). All-or-none processes in learning and retention. *American Psychologist, 19,* 16–25.

Estes, W. K. (1972). Reinforcement in human behavior. *American Scientist, 60,* 723–729.

Feuerstein, R., Rand, Y., Hoffman, M. B., & Miller, R. (1980). *Instructional enrichment: An intervention program for cognitive modifiability.* Baltimore, MD: University Park Press.

Fitts, P. M., & Posner, M. J. (1967). *Human performance.* Belmont, CA: Brooks/Cole.

Flavell, J. H. (1970). Developmental studies of mediated memory. In H. W. Reese & L. P. Lipsitt (Eds.), *Advances in child development and behavior,* Vol. 5. New York: Academic Press.

Flavell, J. H. (1963). *The developmental psychology of Jean Piaget.* Princeton, NJ: Van Nostrand.

Flavell, J. H., & Wellman, H. M. (1977). Metamemory. In R. V. Kail, Jr., & J. W. Hagen (Eds.), *Perspectives on the development of memory and cognition.* Hillsdale, NJ: Erlbaum.

Gagné, E. D. (1985). *The cognitive psychology of school learning.* Boston: Little, Brown.

Gagné, R. M. (1983). Some issues in the psychology of mathematics instruction. *Journal for Research in Mathematics Education, 14,* 7–18.

Gagné, R. M. (1985). *The conditions of learning,* 4th ed. New York: Holt, Rinehart and Winston.

Gagné, R. M. (1984). Learning outcomes and their effects: Useful categories of human performance. *American Psychologist, 39,* 377–385.

Gagné, R. M., Briggs, L. J., & Wager, W. W. (1988). *Principles of instruction design,* 3rd ed. New York: Holt, Rinehart and Winston.

Gartner, A., Kohler, M. G., & Riessman, F. (1971). *Children teach children: Learning by teaching.* New York: Harper & Row.

Gibson, E. J. (1969). *Principles of perceptual learning and development.* New York: Appleton-Century-Crofts.

Gibson, J. J. (1929). The reproduction of visually perceived forms. *Journal of Experimental Psychology, 12,* 1–39.

Gick, M. L. (1986). Problem-solving strategies. *Educational Psychologist, 21*(1&2), 99–120.

Glaser, R. (1961). Learning and the technology of instruction. *AV Communication Review, 9,* 42–55.

Glaser, R. (Ed.). (1971). *The nature of reinforcement.* New York: Academic Press.

Glynn, S. M., & DiVesta, F. J. (1977). Outline and hierarchial organization as aids for study and retrieval. *Journal of Educational Psychology, 69,* 9–14.

Haslerud, G. M. (1973). *Transfer, memory & creativity.* Minneapolis: University of Minnesota Press.

Hebb, D. O. (1972). *A textbook of psychology,* 3rd ed. Philadelphia: Saunders.

Hendrickson, G., & Schroeder, W. H. (1941). Transfer of training in learning to hit a submerged target. *Journal of Educational Psychology, 32,*.205–213.

Higbee, K. L. (1979). Recent research on visual mnemonics. Historical roots and educational fruits. *Review of Educational Research, 49,* 611–630.

Hill, W. F. (1963). *Learning: A survey of psychological interpretations.* San Francisco: Chandler.

Hulse, S. H., Egeth, H., & Deese, J. (1981). *The psychology of learning,* 5th ed. New York: McGraw-Hill.

Jensen, A. R., & Rohwer, W. D., Jr. (1963). Verbal mediation in paired-associate and serial learning. *Journal of Verbal Learning and Verbal Behavior, 1,* 346–352.

Johnson, D. M. (1972). *Systematic introduction to the psychology of thinking.* New York: Harper & Row.

Johnson, D. W., & Johnson, R. T. (1975). *Learning together and alone: Cooperation, competition, and individualization.* Englewood Cliffs, NJ: Prentice Hall.

Jones, B. F., Amiran, M., & Katims, M. (1985). Teaching cognitive strategies and text structures within language arts programs. In J. W. Segal, S. F. Chipman, & R. Glaser (Eds.), *Thinking and learning skills: Relating instruction to research,* Vol. 1. Hillsdale, NJ: Erlbaum.

Jones, B. F., & Hall, J. W. (1982). School applications of the mnemonic keyword method as a study strategy by eighth graders. *Journal of Educational Psychology, 74,* 230–237.

Jones, R. A. (1977). *Self-fulfilling prophecies: Social, psychological, and psychological effects of expectancies.* New York: Halsted Press.

Joyce, B., & Weil, M. (1972). *Models of teaching.* Englewood Cliffs, NJ: Prentice Hall.

Judd, C. H. (1908). The relation of special training to general intelligence. *Educational Review, 36,* 28–42.

Katona, G. (1940). *Organizing and memorizing.* New York: Columbia University Press.

Keller, F. S. (1974). Ten years of personalized instruction. *Teaching of Psychology, 1,* 4–9.

Keller, J. M. (1983). Motivational design of instruction. In C. M. Reigeluth (Ed.), *Instructional-design theories and models: An overview of their current status.* Hillsdale, NJ: Erlbaum.

Keller, J. M. (1984). The use of the ARCS model of motivation in teacher training. In K. Shaw (Ed.), *Aspects of educational technology XVII: Staff development and career updating.* New York: Nichols.

Kiewra, K. A. (1985). Investigating notetaking and review: A depth of processing alternative. *Educational Psychologist, 20*(1), 23–32.

Klatzky, R. L. (1980). *Human memory: Structures and processes,* 2nd ed. San Francisco: Freeman.

Knirk, F. G., & Gustafson, K. L. (1986). *Instructional technology: A systematic approach to education.* New York: Holt, Rinehart and Winston.

Krasner, L., & Ullman, L. P. (1965). *Research in behavior modification: New developments and implications.* New York: Holt, Rinehart and Winston.

Krathwohl, D. R., Bloom, B. S., & Masia, B. B. (1964). *Taxonomy of educational objectives. Handbook II: Affective domain.* New York: McKay.

Kulhavy, R. W., Lee, J. B., & Caterino, L. C. (1985). Conjoint retention of maps and related discourse. *Contemporary Educational Psychology, 10,* 28–37.

Kulhavy, R. W., & Swenson, I. (1975). Imagery instructions and the comprehension of text. *British Journal of Educational Psychology, 45,* 47–51.

LaBerge, D., & Samuels, S. J. (1974). Toward a theory of automatic information processing in reading. *Cognitive Psychology, 6,* 293–323.

Lesser, G. S. (1974). *Children and television.* New York: Random House.

Levin, J. R., & Kaplan, S. A. (1972). Imaginal facilitation of paired-associate learning: A limited generalization? *Journal of Educational Psychology, 63,* 429–432.

Levin, J. R., & Pressley, M. (Eds.). (1986). Special issue: Learning strategies. *Educational Psychologist, 21*(1&2).

Lindahl, L. G. (1945). Movement analysis as an industrial training method. *Journal of Applied Psychology, 29,* 420–436.

Lindsay, P. H., & Norman, D. A. (1977). *Human information processing: An introduction to psychology,* 2nd ed. New York: Academic Press.

Mager, R. F. (1962). *Preparing objectives for instruction.* Belmont, CA: Fearon.

Mager, R. F. (1975). *Developing attitude toward learning,* 2nd ed. Belmont, CA: Fearon.

Martin, B. L., & Briggs, L. J. (1986). *The affective and cognitive domains: Integration for instruction and research.* Englewood Cliffs, NJ: Educational Technology.

McClelland, D. C. (1976). *The achieving society.* New York: Irvington.

McClelland, D. C., Atkinson, J. W., Clark, R. W., & Lowell, E. L. (1953). *The achievement motive.* New York: Appleton-Century-Crofts.

McCombs, B. L. (1981–1982). Transitioning learning strategies research into practice: Focus on the student in technical training. *Journal of Instructional Development, 5,* 10–17.

McKeachie, W. J., Pintrich, P. R., & Lin, Y. Teaching learning strategies. *Educational Psychologist, 20*(3), 153–160.

Meichenbaum, D. H. (1977). *Cognitive behavior modification: An integrative approach.* New York: Plenum.

Merrill, M. D. (1971). *Instructional design: Readings.* Englewood Cliffs, NJ: Prentice Hall.

Merrill, M. D. (1971). Paradigms for psychomotor instruction. In M. D. Merrill (Ed.), *Instructional design: Readings.* Englewood Cliffs, NJ: Prentice Hall.

Miller, G. A. (1956). The magical number seven, plus or minus two: Some limits to our capacity for processing information. *Psychological Review, 63,* 81–97.

Murphy, D. A., & Derry, S. J. (1984, April). *Description of an introductory learning strategies course for the Job Skills Education Program.* Paper presented at the annual meeting of the American Educational Research Association, New Orleans, LA.

Norman, D. A. (1969). *Memory and attention.* New York: Wiley.

Norman, D. A. (Ed.). (1970). *Models of human memory.* New York: Academic Press.

O'Neil, H. F., Jr. (1978). *Learning strategies.* New York: Academic Press.

Paivio, A. (1971). *Imagery and verbal processes.* New York: Holt, Rinehart and Winston.

Peper, R. J., & Mayer, R. E. (1978). Notetaking as a generative activity. *Journal of Educational Psychology, 70,* 514–522.

Peterson, L. R., & Peterson, M. J. (1959). Short-term retention of individual verbal items. *Journal of Experimental Psychology, 58,* 193–198.

Popham, W. J., & Baker, E. L. (1970). *Planning an instructional sequence.* Englewood Cliffs, NJ: Prentice Hall.

Popham, W. J., & Baker, E. L. (1970). *Systematic instruction.* Englewood Cliffs, NJ: Prentice Hall.

Postlethwait, S. N., Novak, J., & Murray, H. (1972). *The audiotutorial approach to learning,* 3rd ed. Minneapolis: Burgess.

Pressley, M., Borkowski, J. G., & O'Sullivan, J. T. (1984). Memory strategy instruction is made of this: Metamemory and durable strategy use. *Educational Psychologist, 19,* 94–107.

Pressley, M., & Levin, J. R. (1983). *Cognitive strategy research: Educational applications.* New York: Springer-Verlag.

Pressley, M., & Levin, J. R. (1983). *Cognitive strategy research: Psychological foundations.* New York: Springer-Verlag.

Reigeluth, C. M. (Ed.). (1983). *Instructional-design theories and models: An overview of their current status.* Hillsdale, NJ: Erlbaum.

Reigeluth, C. M., & Stein, F. S. (1983). The elaboration theory of instruction. In C. M. Reigeluth (Ed.), *Instructional-design theories and models: An overview of their current status.* Hillsdale, NJ: Erlbaum.

Reiser, R. A. (1987). Instructional technology: A history. In R. M. Gagné, (Ed.), *Instructional technology: Foundations.* Hillsdale, NJ: Erlbaum.

Reiser, R. A., & Gagné, R. M. (1983). *Selecting media for instruction.* Englewood Cliffs, NJ: Educational Technology.

Reynolds, J. H., & Glaser, R. (1964). Effects of repetition and spaced review upon retention of a complex learning task. *Journal of Educational Psychology, 55,* 297–308.

Rickards, J., & August, G. J. (1975). Generative underlining strategies in prose recall. *Journal of Educational Psychology, 67,* 860–865.

Rohwer, W. D., Jr. (1974). Elaboration and learning in childhood and adolescence. In H. W. Reese (Ed.), *Advances in child development and behavior.* New York: Academic Press.

Rohwer, W. D., Jr., & Lynch, S. (1966). Semantic constraint in paired-associate learning. *Journal of Educational Psychology, 57,* 271–278.

Romiszowski, A. J. (1974). *The selection and use of instructional media.* London: Kogan Page.

Salomon, G. (1981). *Communication and education: Social and psychological interactions.* Beverly Hills, CA: Sage.

Savell, J. M., Twohig, P. T., & Rachford, D. L. (1986). Empirical status of Feuerstein's "Instrumental Enrichment" (FIE) technique as a method of teaching thinking skills. *Review of Educational Research, 56,* 381–409.

Schramm, G. (1977). *Big media, little media.* Beverly Hills, CA: Sage.

Segal, J. W., Chipman, S. F., & Glaser, R. (1985). *Thinking and learning skills: Relating instruction to research,* Vol. 1. Hillsdale, NJ: Erlbaum.

Shulman, L. S., & Keislar, E. R. (1966). *Learning by discovery: A critical appraisal.* Chicago: Rand McNally.

Singer, R. N. (1980). *Motor learning and human performance,* 3rd ed. New York: Macmillan.

Skinner, B. F. (1968). *The technology of teaching.* New York: Appleton-Century-Crofts.

Spilich, G. J., Vesonder, G. T., Chiesi, H. L., & Voss, J. F. (1979). Text processing of domain-related information for individuals with high and low domain knowledge. *Journal of Verbal Learning and Verbal Behavior, 18,* 275–290.

Tessmer, M., & Driscoll, M. P. (1986). Effects of a diagrammatic display of concept definitions on classification performance. *Educational Communications and Technology Journal, 34,* 195–205.

Thorndike, E. L. (1913). *Educational psychology. Vol. II. The psychology of learning.* New York: Teachers College, Columbia University.

Torgesen, J. K. (1977). The role of nonspecific factors in the task performance of learning disabled children: A theoretical assessment. *Journal of Learning Disabilities, 10,* 27–34.

Travers, R. M. W. (1985). *Essentials of learning,* 5th ed. New York: Macmillan.

Triandis, H. C. (1971). *Attitude and attitude change.* New York: Wiley.

Tulving, E. & Pearlstone, Z. (1966). Availability versus accessibility of information in memory for words. *Journal of Verbal Learning and Verbal Behavior, 5,* 381–391.

Tyler, R. W. (1949). *Basic principles of curriculum and instruction.* Chicago: University of Chicago Press.

Wager, W. W., & Gagné, R. M. (1987). Designing computer-aided instruction. In D. H. Jonassen (Ed.), *Instructional designs for microcomputer courseware.* Hillsdale, NJ: Erlbaum.

Weinstein, C. E. (1982). A metacurriculum for remediating learning strategies deficits in academically unprepared students. In L. Noel & R. Levitz (Eds.), *How to succeed with academically unprepared students.* Iowa City, IA: American College Testing Service.

Weinstein, C. E., & Mayer, R. E. (1985). The teaching of learning strategies, In M. C. Wittrock (Ed.), *Handbook of research on teaching,* 3rd ed. New York: Macmillan.

Wessels, M. G. (1982). *Cognitive psychology.* New York: Harper & Row.

White, R. W. (1959). Motivation reconsidered: The concept of competence. *Psychological Review, 66,* 297–333.

Zimbardo, P. G. (Ed.). (1969). *The cognitive control of motivation.* Glenview, IL: Scott, Foresman.

NAME INDEX

(The pages are underlined for those names that appear in the General References at the end of each chapter.)

Adams, J. A., 34
Amiran, M., 177
Anderson, J. R., 9, 28, 29, 30, 41
Anderson, L. W., 160
Armbruster, B., 145
Atkinson, J. W., 178
Atkinson, R. C., 24
August, G. J., 134
Ausubel, D. P., 89

Baker, E. L., 105, 132
Bandura, A., 65, 66, 70, 81, 98, 99, 105
Barber, L., 161
Bellezza, F. S., 136
Berlyne, D. E., 64
Block, J. H., 160
Bloom, B. S., 58, 61, 94, 105, 160, 171
Borkowski, J. G., 134
Bower, G. H., 19, 41
Bransford, J. D., 19, 41, 167
Briggs, L. J., 19, 41, 61, 62, 84, 105, 132, 166
Brown, A. L., 134
Bruner, J. S., 56, 62

Campione, J. C., 145
Carmichael, L., 32
Carrier, C. A., 137
Caterino, L. C., 7
Chiesi, H. L., 179
Chipman, S. F., 62, 149
Clark, L. W., 178
Conrad, R., 30
Covington, M. V., 96
Crutchfield, R. S., 96

Dansereau, D. F., 139
Davies, L. B., 96
Derry, S. J., 95, 138, 143, 145, 147, 149, 171
Deese, J., 41

DiVesta, F. J., 89
Driscoll, M. P., 89

Egeth, H., 41
Ellson, D. G., 161
Estes, W. K., 25, 38, 71

Feuerstein, R., 145
Fitts, P. M., 62, 99, 101
Fitzgerald, D., 89
Flavell, J. H., 96, 135

Gagné, E. D., 92, 105, 131
Gagné, R. M., 19, 23, 41, 44, 47, 58, 61, 62, 78, 84, 92, 94, 105, 129, 131, 132, 148, 166, 168, 170, 171, 174
Gartner, A., 161
Gibson, E. J., 47
Gibson, J. J., 29, 30
Gick, M. L., 144
Glaser, R., 62, 78, 93, 149
Glynn, S. M., 89
Gustafson, K. L., 174

Hall, J. W., 90
Harris, P., 161
Haslerud, G. M., 37
Hastings, J. T., 61
Hebb, D. O., 27
Hendrickson, G., 36
Higbee, K. L., 136
Hilgard, E. R., 19, 41
Hill, W. F., 19, 41
Hogan, H. F., 32
Hoffman, M. B., 145
Hulse, S. H., 41

Jensen, A. R., 32
Johnson, D. M., 115
Johnson, D. W., 161, 163
Johnson, M. K., 167
Johnson, R. T., 161, 163

Jones, B. F., 90, 145
Jones, R. A., 70
Joyce, B., 174
Judd, C. H., 36

Kaplan, S. A., 32
Katims, M., 177
Katona, G., 32
Keislar, E. R., 93
Keller, F. S., 163
Keller, J. M., 67, 68, 72, 81
Kiewra, K. A., 137
Klatzky, R. L., 19, 28, 41
Knirk, F. G., 174
Kohler, M. G., 161
Krasner, L., 37
Krathwohl, D. R., 58
Kulhavy, R. W., 7, 89

LaBerge, D., 94
Lee, J. B., 7
Lesser, G. S., 69, 81, 87, 168
Levin, J. R., 32, 89, 148, 149
Lin, Y., 145
Lindahl, L. G., 101
Lindsay, P. H., 12, 19
Lowell, E. L., 178
Lynch, S., 32, 89

Madaus, G. F., 61
Mager, R. F., 62
Martin, B. L., 62
Masia, B. B., 58
Mayer, R. E., 137, 149
McClelland, D. C., 65, 81
McCombs, B. L., 144
McKeachie, W. J., 145
Meichenbaum, D. H., 140
Merrill, M. D., 101, 105
Miller, G. A., 31
Miller, R., 145
Murphy, D. A., 95, 138, 143, 145, 147, 149, 171
Murray, H. T., Jr., 174

Norman, D. A., 12, 19, 89
Novak, J., 174

Olton, R. M., 96
O'Neill, H. F., Jr., 62
O'Sullivan, J. T., 134

Paivio, A., 167
Pearlstone, Z., 35

Peper, R. J., 137
Peterson, L. R., 30
Peterson, M. J., 30
Pintrich, P. R., 145
Popham, W. J., 105, 132
Posner, M. J., 62, 99, 101
Postlethwait, S. N., 163, 174
Pressley, M., 89, 134, 143, 148, 149

Rachford, D. L., 145
Rand, Y., 145
Reigeluth, C. M., 19, 41, 68, 109, 174
Reiser, R. A., 162, 168, 174
Reissman, F., 161
Reynolds, J. H., 93
Rickards, J., 134
Rohwer, W. D., 32, 88, 95
Romiszowski, A. J., 174

Salomon, G., 174
Samuels, S. J., 94
Savell, J. M., 145
Schramm, W., 174
Schroeder, W. H., 36
Segal, J. W., 62, 149
Shiffrin, R. M., 24
Shulman, L. S., 93
Singer, R. N., 62, 101
Skinner, B. F., 11, 26, 38
Smiley, S. S., 134
Spilich, G. J., 90
Stein, F. S., 109
Swenson, I., 89

Tessmer, M., 89
Thorndike, E. L., 10, 11
Titus, A., 137
Torgeson, J. K., 143
Triandis, H. C., 62
Tulving, E., 35
Twohig, P. T., 145
Tyler, R. W., 132

Ullman, L. P., 38

Vesonder, G. T., 90
Voss, J. F., 90

Wager, W. W., 19, 41, 61, 105, 132, 166, 170

Walter, A. A., 32
Weinstein, C. E., 136, 144, 149
Wellman, H. M., 135
Wessels, M. G., 41

White, R. W., 25, 65, 81

Zimbardo, P. G., 64

SUBJECT INDEX

Achievement motive, 65
Advance organizer, 89
ARCS model, 68
   attention, 68–69
   confidence, 70
   relevance, 69–70
   satisfaction, 70–71
Assessment of performance, in lesson
   planning, 125
Attention
   affective strategies, 139–140
   learner strategy, 134–135
   learning process, 26–28
   sustaining, 72–73
Attitudes, 57–58
   conditions for learning, 97–99
   prerequisites, 115–116

Chunking, in short-term memory, 30–31
Cognitive strategies, 55–57
   conditions for learning, 95–97
   prerequisites, 115
Computer-based instruction, instructional events, 170–171
Concepts
   concrete, 49–50
   defined, 50–51
Conditions for learning, 83–104
   attitudes, 97–99
   chunking, 88
   cognitive strategies, 95–97
   cues for recall, 90–91
   elaboration, 90
   instruction, 102
   intellectual skills, 91–95
   motor skills, 99–102
   practice, spaced reviews, 93–94
   providing a context, 88–90
   recall of subordinate skills, 92–93
   relation to outcomes, 85

   variety of contexts, 94
   verbal information, 85–91
Confidence
   affective strategies, 140–141
   installing as motivation, 75–77
Curiosity motive, 64–65

Discriminations, 47–49

Elaboration, 90
   instructional planning, 109–110
Encoding (*see* Semantic encoding)
Epitome, elaboration model, 109–110
Events of instruction (*see* Instructional
   events)
Executive control, 24
Expectancies, 24

Feedback
   lesson planning, 124–125
   motor skill learning, 101–102
   phase in learning, 37–38

Imagery, 89
Instruction
   class, 152–157
   comparison, three modes, 159
   delivery, 151–165, 172–173
   events, 118–127
   individualized systems, 162–163
   individual student, 157–163
   planning, 107–127
   prerequisite sequence, 111–116
   relation to learning processes, 127, 129
   self-learner, 127–128, 130
   tutorial, 158–161
   using media, 165–173
   variety of modes, 163–164

Instructional events
    adapting to class, 157
    choosing for lesson, 130–131
    class setting, 153–157
    comparison, instructional modes, 159
    computer-based instruction, 170–171
    eliciting performance, 155
    enhancing retention, transfer, 155–156
    influence on learning processes, 39–41
    learning guidance, 154
    lesson, 118
    providing feedback, 155
    stimulating recall, 154
Instructional planning, 107–127
    checklist of features, 113
    choosing events, 130–131
    course, 108–109
    elaboration, 109–110
    events in class setting, 153–157
    events of instruction, 118–127
    lesson, 116–127
    multiple goals, 110–111
    sequence, 111–116
Intellectual skills, 47–55
    complexity, 48
    concrete concepts, 49–50
    defined concepts, 50–51
    discriminations, 47–49
    higher-order rules, 52–54
    prerequisites, 111–113
    problem solving, 53
    rules, 51–52

Keyword method, 89–90

Learner control, increasing confidence,
    76–77
Learner strategies, 133–148
    acquisition, 141–144
    affective, 139–141
    age-dependent, 143
    attention, 134–135
    encoding, 136–137
    implications for teaching, 144–147
    internal processing, 134
    monitoring, 138
    retrieval, 137
    short-term storage, 135–136
    simple vs. complex, 142–143
    specific vs. general, 143–144
Learning
    conditions, 83–104
    knowledge about, 4–6
    nature of, 2–4
    processes, 21–41

    teacher's task, 2
    theory, 10–17
Learning goals, multiple, 110–111
    learning guidance, lesson planning,
    122–124
Learning outcomes, 43–61
    attitudes, 57–58
    categories of human capabilities, 61
    categorizing, 84
    cognitive strategies, 55–57
    intellectual skills, 47–55
    motor skills, 58–59
    types, 44
    verbal information, 44–47

Learning processes, 22–24
    attention, 26–28
    chunking, 30–31
    feedback, 37–38
    generalization, 36–37
    influence of external events, 39–41
    instruction, 38–41
    motivation, 25–26
    performance, 36–37
    rehearsal, 30–31
    relation to structures, 23
    search and retrieval, 35
    selective perception, 28–29
    semantic encoding, 31–33
    sequence, 24–38
    storage in long-term memory, 33–34
Learning research, 5–9
    controls, 9
    example, 6–7
    principle, 9
    reliability, 7–8
    validity, 8
Learning theory
    behaviorist, 10–12
    information-processing, 12–13
    modern cognitive, 12–15
    reinforcement, 11–12
    Thorndike's, 10–11
    usefulness, 15–17

Media
    audio tape cassettes, 169–170
    computer-based, 170–172
    pictures in instruction, 166–167
    television, 167–169
    using for instruction, 165–173
Memory
    long-term, 33–34
    short-term, 29–31
Mental effort, 66–67
Mnemonics, 89

Motivation for learning, 63–80
   achievement, 65
   curiosity, 64–65
   establishing, 25–26
   incentive, 25
   mental effort, 66–67
   model, ARCS, 67–71
   self-efficacy, 65–66
   sources, 64–67
   strategies, 139–141
   techniques, 72–79
Motor skills, 58–59
   conditions for learning, 99–102
   prerequisites, 116

Perception (*see* Selective perception)
Prerequisites
   design of topics, courses, 114
   enabling and supportive, 113
   sequence, in instruction, 111–116

Rehearsal, in short-term memory, 30–31
Relevance
   affective strategies, 140
   in motivation, 73–75
Retention, in lesson planning, 125–126
Retrieval, strategies, 137
Rules, 51–52
   area problem, 53
   higher-order, 52–54

Satisfaction
   affective strategies, 141

feedback, 78
   generalization, 78–79
   motivational factor, 77–79
Search and retrieval, 35
Selective perception, 28–29
Self-efficacy, 65–66
Self-instruction, 161–163
   learning, 127–128, 130
Semantic encoding, 31–33
   condition for learning, 88–89
   lesson planning, 122–124
   strategies, 136–137
Short-term storage, 29–31
   strategies, 135–136

Transfer
   learning, 36–37
   lesson planning, 125–126
Tutoring
   effects, 160
   student, 160–161

Verbal information
   conditions for learning, 85–91
   distinctive features, 87–88
   functions, 45–47
   prerequisites, 114
Verbs, in learning outcome statements,
      85–87